W0017328

MYTHS AND MYSTERIES

OF

ALASKA

MYTHS AND MYSTERIES SERIES

MYTHS AND MYSTERIES

OF
ALASKA

TRUE STORIES
OF THE UNSOLVED AND UNEXPLAINED

CHERRY LYON JONES

Guilford, Connecticut

For Galen

To buy books in quantity for corporate use
or incentives, call **(800) 962-0973**
or e-mail **premiums@GlobePequot.com.**

Copyright © 2013 by Morris Book Publishing, LLC

ALL RIGHTS RESERVED. No part of this book may be reproduced or transmitted in any form by any means, electronic or mechanical, including photocopying and recording, or by any information storage and retrieval system, except as may be expressly permitted in writing from the publisher. Requests for permission should be addressed to Globe Pequot Press, Attn: Rights and Permissions Department, PO Box 480, Guilford, CT 06437.

Map by Alena Joy Pearce © Morris Book Publishing, LLC
Project Editor: Lauren Brancato
Layout: Mary Ballachino and Justin Marciano

Library of Congress Cataloging-in-Publication Data is available on file.

ISBN 978-0-7627-7222-3

Printed in the United States of America

10 9 8 7 6 5 4 3 2 1

CONTENTS

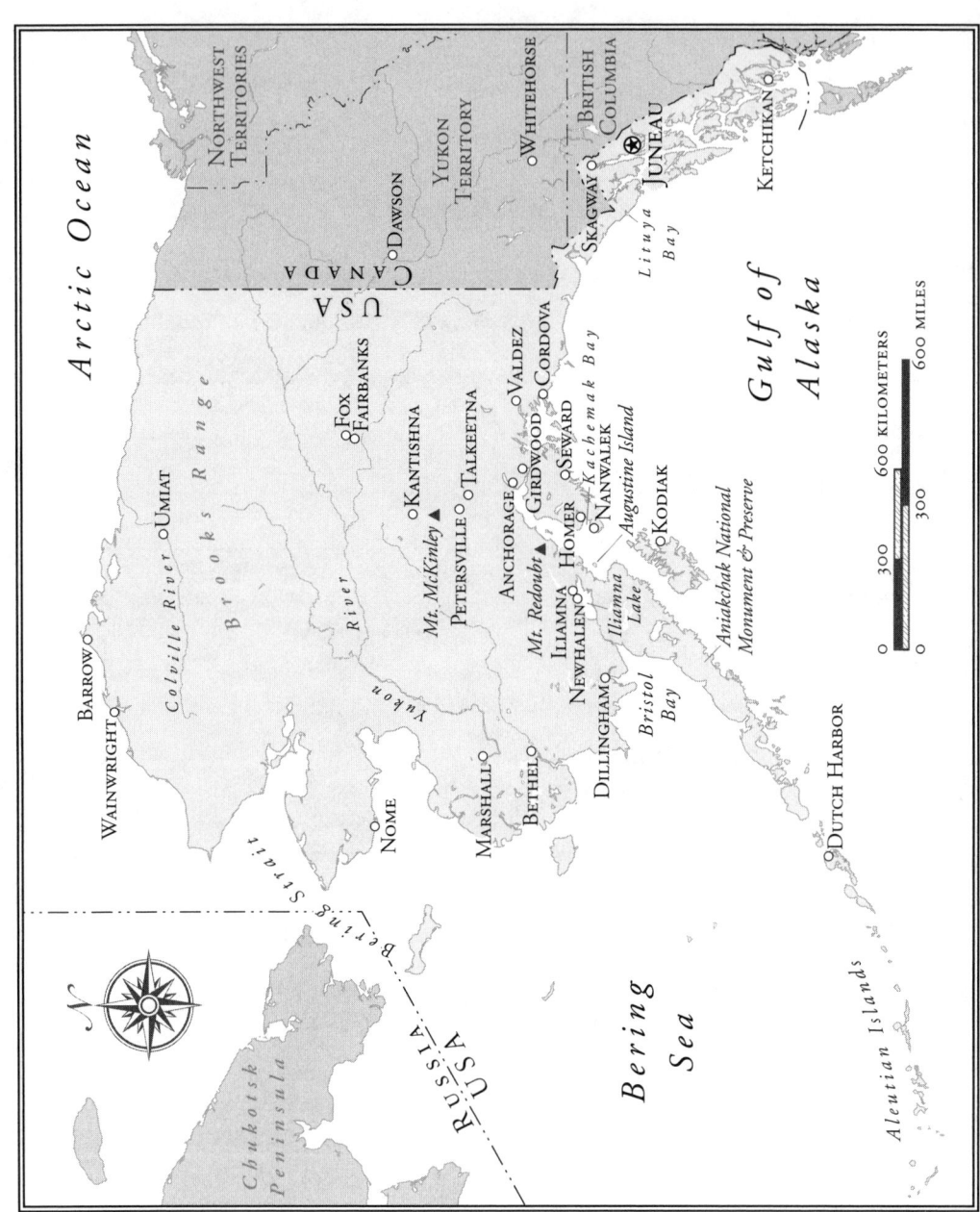

ACKNOWLEDGMENTS

When an author sits down to put words on a blank sheet, she (or he) is never working alone. Assistance and encouragement come from many directions. Here are some of the directions from which it came for me, and I am exceedingly grateful.

Thanks to the Kachemak Bay Writers' Conference in Homer, Alaska, for inspiration, and to the Thursday Afternoon Homer Writers' Group for encouragement.

Thanks to Sherry Simpson, for alerting me to the JAL 1628 story (and for her workshops at the conference).

Thanks to Greg Christian, Brad Joseph, and Ed Schlief for sharing their "Hairy Man" encounters with me, and to my son Dave Lyon for introducing me to them.

Thanks to my neighbor Dave Hanrahan for telling me about the Big Fish in Lake Iliamna.

Thanks to Dr. Daniel H. Shain of Rutgers University for reading the "Ice Worms" chapter to be sure that I got the science "right."

Thanks to Dottie and Mike Cline for advice regarding the "Little People" chapter.

Thanks to Margaret Cysewski of the US Army Cold Regions Research and Engineering Laboratory for the great tour of the Permafrost Tunnel in Fox, Alaska.

Thanks to the librarians at the Homer Library, especially Amy Gordon, for obtaining those many books by interlibrary loan!

Roberta Sheldon, widow of legendary Alaska bush pilot, Don Sheldon, wrote an amazing book about the Cache Creek murders. For six years Roberta pored over old court documents, obituaries, letters, photographs, newspapers, mining claims, contracts, maps, personal diaries, and memoirs. She interviewed dozens of old-timers. (Her late husband had, as a very young man, actually worked for Frank Jenkins, one of the victims, during that summer before the murders.) Her research resulted in a comprehensive study of the still unsolved murders, and a "page-turner" of a book. I couldn't have done my chapter without it.

Thanks, certainly, to my editor, Tracee Williams, for her patience and suggestions.

Thanks to my daughter, Becky Lyon Van Sickle, and my sister, Betty Trout, for proofreading and encouragement.

And, certainly, thanks to my husband, Fred, not only for the explanation of "pilot lingo" for the UFO chapter and for excellent editing, but also for his patience and good help, especially as each deadline neared!

INTRODUCTION

The first thing to realize about Alaska is that it is huge! If a map of Alaska were superimposed over a same-scale map of the contiguous United States, the southwest end of the Aleutian Island chain would touch the Pacific Ocean down to about San Diego, the far north town of Barrow would reach the Canadian border somewhere in Minnesota, and the tip of the Southeast corner would meet the Atlantic Ocean off of South Carolina. Of course, it is the biggest state in the Union.

The area covered by Alaska is more than 660,000 square miles, more than twice the size of Texas, the second biggest state in the Union. But the population of the whole state is only about 723,000, and more than half of those people live in the Anchorage Metropolitan Area. So that means that there are vast areas, thousands and thousands of square miles, where there are no people living at all. There are places in Alaska that have never been seen by human eyes! Who knows what strange events happen unobserved or what unknown species might be running amok in the mountains?

So what is out there in the Alaska wilderness? There are stories told of strange happenings on the tundra. Miners who have spent months and months alone in the creeks come back into civilization with descriptions of unearthly creatures seen around their cabins. Hunters hear wild screams in the night. Children have nightmares of strange faces looking in through the windows.

Alaska is full of myths. The native people have long told stories that explain the unexplainable. The stories are about unseen creatures, or about phenomena seen but not understood. The pioneers and settlers that came into Alaska from other parts of the world brought their stories and myths, too. And modern inventions and explanations moved into the stories, changing their characters, perhaps, but not their entertainment value or their deeper meanings.

Alaska is also very mysterious. When the volcano Novarupta erupted in 1912, it was the largest eruption of the century and formed a valley full of wispy fumaroles, The Valley of Ten Thousand Smokes! The plumes of smoke wafted into the air for many years, but have since disappeared. However, earthquakes are an everyday occurrence, and residents of the Alaska Peninsula and the Aleutians are always alert to the warning wisps of smoke from any of the nearby volcanoes.

In the northern part of the state, the freezing and thawing of the ground tips buildings and mangles roads. The permafrost holds surprises that are thousands, even millions, of years old.

Alaska is so big that it is more like a whole country. There are six unofficial regions in the state, each one very different from any other.

The Southeast region is that strip of land along the Inside Passage, where cruise ships bring tourists from the Lower 48. They travel past (and usually visit) the towns of Ketchikan, Haines, and Skagway, as well as Juneau, the capital of Alaska, and the island of Sitka, which was the first capital. Care is suggested when exploring the rainforests . . . the Hairy Man may be lurking there.

The South Central region is the most populated part of the state. It includes the city of Anchorage and the Matanuska Valley to the north, where the huge pumpkins and cabbages are grown. To the south it includes the Kenai Peninsula, with the towns of Seward, where many cruise ships dock, on the east side, and Homer, the "Halibut Capital of the World" on the west. Wary residents keep their eyes on the skies for smoke escaping Redoubt, or Augustine, or even Iliamna!

The Interior region is, as it sounds, sort of in the middle of the state. It includes the city of Fairbanks, as well as Denali National Park. Mount McKinley, the highest spot in North America at 20,320 feet, is located there. Native Athabascans named the overpowering mountain Denali, meaning "High One," or "Great One."

The North Slope region is covered with tundra and underlain by permafrost. Who knows what secrets are hidden within the frozen ground? The area includes the Prudhoe Bay Oil Field and the Arctic National Refuge. The northwest part of the state, just above the Seward Peninsula and including Kotzebue, is usually considered a part of this region also.

The Southwest region includes the island of Kodiak and the Yukon–Kuskokwim Delta and Lake Iliamna. The town of Bethel is in the southwest, and following up the coast at the very top of the region is the Seward Peninsula and the town of Nome. The Big Fish swims silently in Lake Iliamna, and Ircenrraats might be near.

The Aleutian Island region consists of more than three hundred small volcanic islands stretching 1,200 miles out into the Pacific Ocean. The largest community on the "chain" is Unalaska, which contains Dutch Harbor, on the island of Unalaska. The very tip of the chain is actually on the other side of the International Date Line, but the line was drawn 180 degrees west so that all of Alaska would be on the same legal day. Because of this, Alaska is actually not only the most northern state in the Union, but also the most western and the most eastern! Now that's mysterious!

It is sometimes difficult for the newcomer, the "cheechako," or the visitor, to learn where the important places in Alaska are located.

The helpful "sourdough," or long-time resident, will offer this advice:

Hold out your right hand, with the thumb pointed down at the floor. Point your index finger straight ahead. Bend under your middle, ring, and little fingers at the second joint. Now, you have a map of Alaska. In the middle of your thumbnail is Ketchikan. About halfway up your thumb is Juneau. About a quarter of an inch above the curve between your thumb and forefinger is Anchorage. Slightly more than halfway up your hand and a little toward your wrist is Fairbanks. At the top of your hand, halfway between your wrist and your little finger, is Barrow. Following on around your fingers, Kotzebue is on the joint of your little finger. Nome sits at the bended tip of your ring finger and Bethel is nestled there at the tip of your middle finger. Halfway along your index finger is Unalaska, and at the very tip of your fingernail is Attu.

Congratulations! You have mastered the Alaska Hand.

For a handful of Alaska myths and mysteries, keep reading!

CHAPTER 1

Kah Lituya Strikes!

The Tlingit canoes traveled swiftly toward the small open-
ing at the mouth of Lituya Bay leading out to the wild
Alaskan ocean waters. The men paddled furiously in order to
move through the current that raced in and out of the bay with
each tide. But suddenly, Kah Lituya, the Man of Lituya, came
out of the underwater cave where he lived and grabbed one side
of the waves that roared across the mouth. He ordered his slaves,
the bears, and the Land Otter Men, to grab the waves from the
other side, and they vigorously shook and shook the waters, as if
they were tossing the canoes on a blanket.

The villagers watched in horror from their safety along the
inner shores of the bay as the warriors were tossed into the raging waters and drowned. They would search the rocky beaches
and hope to find the bodies of their loved ones so as to perform
the rites that would send them to a pleasant afterlife. The bodies not found would revert to Kah Lituya, where he would turn
them into his bear slaves and send them wandering the shores

that surround Lituya Bay to watch for more incoming canoes that could be tossed on the blanket. Some of the souls would turn into Land Otter Men, spirits who had the shape of a man with long hair, a round mouth, and an otter's tail, and possessed similar powers of a shaman.

Lituya Bay is a small seven-mile-long and two-mile-wide inlet on the west coast of Glacier Bay National Park, at the base of the Fairweather Mountain Range. At the head of the bay are two immense glaciers; Lituya Glacier stretches out toward the north arm coming into the bay, and North Crillon Glacier toward the south arm. In the center of the bay is Cenotaph Island. From above the inlet resembles a whale, with its flukes attached to the glaciers at the head of the bay and Cenotaph Island its eye looking out toward the open sea.

No one knows just when or how many warriors and canoes have met their demise because they were caught by Kah Lituya. But there are many legends and even one in which the numbers of men lost and the date can be authenticated.

Chilkat and Hoon-ah Tlingits often traveled in their canoes along the west coast to trade for copper at Yakatat. One spring, a large party, which included three chiefs, turned their vessels toward Lituya Bay. Four canoes were overturned in the deadly waves at the mouth of the bay and many people, including one of the chiefs, drowned. While the survivors mourned their lost companions, two large ships came into the bay. The Tlingits had never seen such large ships, so they thought these apparitions were their creator, Raven. When the ships lowered the sails and the crew climbed about in the rigging, the watchers on shore thought that they were seeing the big birds lower their wings and small crows fly around them. One family dressed in masks launched a war canoe, but it was overturned in the waves and they struggled back to shore to safety. Finally one old, almost blind man volunteered to go out alone and investigate. He was welcomed on board and given gifts, which he brought back to the waiting Tlingits. Upon discovering the "birds" were actually trading ships, they boarded and traded with the visitors, profitably for both sides. The oral tradition concludes that the big ships stayed in the bay until two of their smaller boats were wrecked and all the men in them were drowned.

That legend was told to ethnographer G. T. Emmons almost exactly one hundred years after the French explorer, Jean-Francois de Galaup, Comte La Perouse, documented the same story in his ships' logs regarding his visit to Lituya Bay in 1786.

King Louis XVI of France had sent La Perouse on the "greatest of all voyages" to explore the northern Pacific, check in on trade with China, and find the Northwest Passage back across Canada. By the time they approached the west coast of Alaska and ended up in Lituya Bay, the expedition had successfully rounded the Cape of Good Hope in January and had many adventures recorded in the logs along the way.

Because of the shape of the mouth of Lituya Bay, the currents are very strong. They have since been measured at a speed of 13.8 miles per hour. La Perouse had anchored near the island in the bay and was conducting research about the area. He sent three small boats to survey the spit at the mouth of the bay. The boats were caught in the swift tidal currents, and, although one was able to escape by frantic rowing, the two other boats and twenty-one men were lost in the waves.

La Perouse erected a small monument on the island, with a plaque that read READER, WHOEVER THOU ART, MINGLE YOUR TEARS WITH OURS. It was La Perouse who named the island Cenotaph, meaning "a tomblike monument to someone buried elsewhere."

Kah Lituya also struck with another sort of wave. The Old Man would send a huge wave coming from the far head of the bay, washing over the land before disappearing through the mouth into the wide sea. One Tlingit legend tells of a woman who went up the hillside from her village to pick berries. Two hunters from the same village were hunting in the mountains and saw a huge landslide descend into the water and force a huge wave through the bay. On their return the three found their entire village washed away and the bodies of their clansmen draped over the trees that remained.

Eventually the Tlingits moved away from the bay, visiting only in the summer, for fishing and berry picking, leaving no native villages behind in Lituya Bay.

By the end of the nineteenth century, the Gold Rush came to the bay, with miners working the sands along the mouth of the bay and a number of mines started in the area. Perhaps showing his displeasure at these turns of events, in 1899 Kah Lituya sent two-hundred-foot-high waves through the bay that washed away a mine and the miners on the shore. Because extracting gold was dangerous and unprofitable, the miners drifted away to other sites and occupations.

In 1917 a former miner, James Huscroft, came to Cenotaph Island and settled there, building a cabin and outbuildings and planting a garden. Although he lived alone on the island for many years, making just one trip into Juneau each year for supplies, he was far from a recluse. Huscroft loved company, and his cabin became quite the social center for fishermen, miners, mountain climbers, and any other travelers who braved the waves at the mouth of the bay.

Huscroft and one of his visitors were among the survivors to experience and describe the notable wave that occurred in 1936. At the time, Huscroft was entertaining Bernard Allen, who had finally persuaded Huscroft to let him visit the fabled bay. Early on the morning of October 27, the two men were awakened by a roar like "the drone of one hundred airplanes at low altitude." Water on the floor of the cabin sent them scurrying outside for higher ground. As it grew lighter they were able to see a huge wave approaching the island from the head of the bay. As they watched they saw three consecutive waves, each larger than the other, sweep across the island.

On that same day two other men, Nick Larson and Fred Frederickson, were anchored near the north shore of Lituya Bay, on their fishing boat, the *Mine*. Before sunrise they heard a loud, steady roar. The weather was clear, and they could begin to see a huge wall of water coming down from the head of the bay. They started toward Cenotaph Island, then turned toward the huge wall of water and were hit by the first wave. It lifted the boat about fifty feet above the surface, and the wave appeared to be fifty more feet taller on both sides. The water on the other side of the wall was below normal, and with each successive wave the crest was higher and the water on the other side lower than normal. After the three waves had passed, the waves gradually returned to normal. Remarkably, the two men managed to keep the boat upright and rode through the waves.

When Huscroft and Allen returned to the cabin, they found it in shambles. The water had washed through the inside up to the windowsills. The rich garden soil that Huscroft had built up over the years was completely washed away, the root cellar was full and ruined, and his outbuildings and dock were gone. The wave also took away Huscroft's spirit. Although he lived for another two years on the island, he never rebuilt the outbuildings or had another garden.

Anecdotal evidence, as well as measuring the tree lines, indicated that the highest 1936 wave was about 490 feet high. There has been a great deal of research done by Forest Service personnel, United States Geologic Survey geologists, and others, to determine the cause of the 1936 waves. Several theories were proposed, such as the sudden breaking of a glacier lake ice dam, an avalanche or rockslide,

Lituya Bay in 1958, after being swept by the biggest wave ever recorded

PLATE 3-B IN US GEOLOGICAL SURVEY. PROFESSIONAL PAPER 354-C. 1960.
COURTESY OF US GEOLOGICAL SURVEY PHOTOGRAPHIC LIBRARY, ID.
MILLER, D. J. 1278.S.

giant berg breaking from a glacier, or an earthquake. However, there is no agreement on the cause, so perhaps it was Kah Lituya and his bear slaves and Land Otter Men up to their mischief again.

It was the granddaddy of all the waves that started out at the head of Lituya Bay in 1958 that has the distinction of being the largest one ever recorded. On July 9 of that year, a group of salmon fishing trawlers was working out on the "Fairweather Grounds" in the Gulf of Alaska. Three of the boats traveled into Lituya Bay and anchored there for the night. Howard Ulrich and his seven-year-old son, Howard Jr., in the trawler, *Edrie*, were settled in just to the south of Cenotaph Island, a small spot of land in the center of the bay. Shortly after 10:00 p.m. Ulrich was awakened by a sharp pull on the anchor. A mammoth earthquake was causing wild disorder all up and down the coast.

Avalanches poured into Lituya Bay, and as Ulrich watched in amazement, he saw the snowcapped tops of the giant mountains of the Fairweather Range twist and shake! Giant boulders and clouds of snow flew off the mountains and rained down their sides.

Suddenly he heard an earsplitting noise as an enormous wave rose from the head of the bay and rushed right toward Cenotaph Island. He threw a life jacket onto his son, let his tow chain out completely and drove the *Edrie* directly into the wave. He shouted into his radio, "All hell has broken loose in here! I think we've had it. . . . Good-bye."

The force snapped the tow chain and miraculously Ulrich and his son rode the wave, coming out on the other side of it amid a slew of ripped out whole trees, ice chunks, rocks, and other debris.

Of the other two boats in the bay that night, one was picked up by the wave and thrown across the mouth of the bay toward the open water at an estimated eighty feet over the treetops, then dropped into the Gulf of Alaska. As it began to sink the couple aboard was able to make it into a small dinghy where they were rescued. The other boat was not so lucky. No trace of it was ever found.

The gigantic wave through which Ulrich skillfully maneuvered the *Edrie* had washed over the headland next to Lituya

Glacier at an unbelievable height of 1,740 feet. This "mega-wave" was twice the height of Hoover Dam, and taller than the Empire State Building!

Don J. Miller, of the United States Geological Survey, had been interested in the huge waves in Lituya Bay for some time. By studying the evidence he had actually estimated that there had been at least three huge waves prior to 1936. Besides the two-hundred-foot wave in 1899, he documented one in 1874 and another in 1853 or 1854. As luck would have it, Miller was actually in Alaska when the 1958 wave hit the bay. He was able to fly over the bay the next day and take several aerial photographs. They clearly show the height of the wave as it washed down the bay, totally stripping the landscape of all trees, bushes, and other vegetation, cutting a wide swath above the water, before washing over the spit at the mouth of the bay and dissipating in the Gulf of Alaska.

In 1960 Miller wrote a paper for the USGS, "Giant Waves in Lituya Bay, Alaska." He suggested several possible causes for the wave, including some that had been suggested as reasons for the 1936 wave. Miller again suggested the "sudden draining of an ice-dammed lake," as well as sudden movement along the fault at the base of the Fairweather Range, avalanche or landslide, movement along a glacier front, or a tsunami in the ocean. He even mentioned ideas that had caused other waves in other places, such as a falling meteorite.

Miller predicted future giant waves in Lituya Bay. He wrote in the 1960 paper that although giant waves have occurred in the bay at least five times in the last 105 years, the odds against one occurring on any given day are about nine thousand to one. Nevertheless, he believed that giant waves will happen, and that anyone entering the bay should be aware of the danger.

As in years past, fishermen will continue to fish the Fairweather Grounds and seek refuge from storms in Lituya Bay. Mountain climbers will continue to start their treks from its banks. Adventurers will continue to make their way over the rough entry of the bay to its calm waters.

They will do well to remember what Don Miller also wrote in his 1960 paper.

"In addition . . . there may be at least one other mechanism, not yet identified, that has generated one or more giant waves in Lituya Bay in the past and might do so again in the future."

Could that "one other mechanism" possibly be Kah Lituya?

CHAPTER 2

Baychimo, *Phantom of the Arctic*

In August of 1933, the seventy-foot-long, two-masted schooner *Trader* ran up against her first ice cake earlier than usual on this route. Ira Rank, her owner, had hoped to make the five-hundred-mile trip from Nome to Barrow in five days, but now they were just rounding Point Lay, and having to travel cautiously. They managed to make about twelve miles before the barrier thickened and they had to anchor for the night surrounded by ice. The gale that came up during the night then forced the little ship and the ice back almost to Point Lay again.

Rank, Captain Pete Palsson, and his brother, Kari, engineer and chief cook, made this trip every year to trade with the Eskimos who lived along the northern Alaska shore. But this year they had a special guest on board. Self-taught botanist Isobel Wylie Hutchison was forty-four years old when she traveled from her home in Scotland in pursuit of Arctic flora specimens to enlarge her collection and those of some British academic institutions. The Hudson's Bay Company ship on which she planned to travel from Nome to Barrow was out of service when she arrived in Nome, so she found herself traveling on the *Trader*.

As they rode out the stormy weather behind a sand bar in a shallow lagoon, conversation drifted to possibilities on the trip ahead.

"I wonder if we shall meet *Baychimo* this year?" said Kari.

"*Baychimo!*" answered Ira. "Why I guess she is over to Siberia long ago."

Isobel's curiosity was immediately piqued by the men's comments and she wanted to know all about this mysterious ship that they referred to as a "ghost derelict."

Baychimo was originally the German ship *Angermanalfven,* built in Sweden in 1915. She was designed to ply the icy waters between Sweden and Germany in the northern Baltic Sea. The ship was relinquished to the British as part of the German reparations after World War I, then purchased from Britain and renamed by the Hudson's Bay Company in 1921.

For the first couple of years the 230-foot long 1,300-ton steamship traveled the ports of northeastern Canada and the northern coast of Siberia. In 1923 she began her yearly voyages along the northern coast of Alaska and sometimes as far to the east as Victoria Island, in Canada's Northwest Territory. She was engaged in the Hudson's Bay Company business of hunting, trapping, and trading with the Eskimos for furs and oils from sea lions and polar bears. The voyages were always treacherous, and the work could only be done during the brief Arctic summers.

Initially *Baychimo* was based in Androssan, Scotland, where she would undergo maintenance during the winter. Then in early spring she would set off across the Atlantic, through the Panama Canal, up the coast to Vancouver, British Columbia, and on north to Alaska. Then her home port was changed to Vancouver, departing from there for her trips along the northern coasts.

Near the end of her second summer on this schedule, she was abruptly dispatched back to the waters around Barrow to assist in rescuing another Hudson's Bay ship, the *Lady Kindersley*, which was trapped in the pack ice nearby. Although unable to actually reach the ship and save her, *Baychimo* picked up her crew, which had been able to trek across the ice to a smaller ship, and transported them safely back to Vancouver. The *Lady Kindersley* herself, complete with her valuable cargo, was a total loss, crushed and destroyed by the relentless sea ice.

On July 7, 1931, *Baychimo*, bedecked for departure with festive flags, took off from Vancouver, bound for her tenth voyage through the Arctic waters. The voyage was dogged by bad weather from the beginning, running into rain, fog, and headwinds all the way between Victoria, British Columbia, and Unalaska, in the Aleutian Island Chain. The steering gear had been damaged by the storms, and they had to drop anchor at Nome, on the northwest coast of Alaska, before they could continue the journey. Captain Sydney Cornwall took a motor launch into Nome to fetch welders to repair the damage.

On July 26, a scant three weeks into the trip, *Baychimo* reached the ice pack, about ten miles south of Wainwright. From there she struggled through the ice, sometimes making several miles headway, then being pushed back those same miles when the wind changed and the ice moved back in around them. Captain Cornwall urged his ship on through the ice in order to reach Barrow. Finally, after being hampered in forward movement for days by ice floes, *Baychimo* dropped anchor in Barrow on August 21.

The 1972 edition of the Canadian Coast Guard book on navigating through the ice recommends that vessels traveling east across the Beaufort Sea pass Point Barrow no later than mid- to late July. Returning west, it is recommended that the latest date to pass through is the end of September. Now *Baychimo* was a full month past that suggested date traveling east. If she encountered any problems at all during the next leg of her journey, she would certainly be courting disaster on the way back. Captain Cornwall made arrangements so that, rather than travel all the way to Cambridge Bay, he could take the ship only as far as the Coppermine terminal. There he would unload the rest of his supplies to be taken to their destinations by small schooners. Even then, as luck would have it, there was no luck. The next several weeks were more of the same struggle through ice floes, and it was already September 9 before Captain Cornwall was able to set the ship's course back toward the west.

So back through the ice floes *Baychimo* traveled. The trip to Herschel Island was uneventful, and the weather reports from there for the next four hundred miles to Barrow were favorable. Unfortunately, the reports were inaccurate, and the ship again began to encounter stormy weather. After taking on fresh reindeer meat from some local Eskimos, who had kayaked out to the ship while it anchored near Barrow, *Baychimo* started pushing her way through the ice toward Wainwright. However, within twenty miles of that destination, the ship ground to a halt, stopped atop another ice cake, and was surrounded by constantly shifting and roaring pack ice.

On this trip out, the ship had several Hudson's Bay employees along as passengers. They all were eager to proceed to Vancouver, but especially the Western Arctic manager, Richard Bonnycastle, who planned to be married immediately upon his return. But the pack ice around the ship now proved to be more than an ordinary delay. As they waited for a northeast wind that might move the ice and provide a lead, or stretch of open water, the fear became great that they might have to winter over in the ice. By now the ice was so thick that it reached to the shore and provided a base so that dog teams were able to come right up to the ship. The men began making preparations for spending the winter. While some of them off-loaded materials from the ship to use in building a habitable structure on shore, others searched the shoreline every day for driftwood and pieces of old whaling ships that could be burned for heat in the structure. What little coal that was left on *Baychimo* was also taken off for use on land.

In early October Captain Cornwall gave the official command to abandon ship, and the entire personnel carried much of the rest of their belongings and other supplies that could be used on land, and moved into the fifteen-by-forty-five-foot wooden cabin.

Arrangements had been made with Nome for small airplanes to come and take the passengers and ten of the crew off to Nome, where they could catch the *Victoria* and be taken to Vancouver. On October 15, two small planes arrived and were able to take seven passengers, including the grateful Bonnycastle, plus the company books and records into Kotzebue. They returned when the weather improved and eventually ferried all of the selected men to Nome in time to catch their ship.

Seventeen men remained on shore prepared to spend the winter and keep tabs on *Baychimo* until it could be salvaged in the spring. The building where they would stay had been constructed from canvas and wood taken from the ship's cargo, as well as large beams and the hatch covers of the ship itself. They had repositioned the wireless equipment from *Baychimo* to the building. The radio operator, A. F. Jamieson, was able to keep in contact with the outside throughout their time there, judiciously using power from the generator that was kept running by use of wood gathered along the shore. They had plenty of food, some taken from the ship, some brought by the small planes from Nome, and some provided by the inhabitants of Wainwright. Kerosene lamps were used for light, and the men were quite comfortable, with lots of books to read and card games to play. Captain Cornwall had purchased a wood-burning stove in Wainwright and the outside of the structure had been insulated with large ice and snow blocks, so the cabin was adequately heated. The men could see the ship, and occasionally were able to travel out to it and recover other items that they might use.

Then a winter gale blasted through the area on November 24. The men huddled inside their housing to wait out the storm. For two days the men could hear the wind howling and the ice groaning, grinding, and scraping. Finally, it was safe to go outside and the men were astonished to see that *Baychimo* was nowhere within sight. Where she had been there now stood a huge pile of sea ice! They searched up the coast for fifteen miles, and continued to comb the area for several days, but no sign of their ship could they see. It was assumed that the ice had piled on top of the ship and sunk her, but not even a piece of wreckage was anywhere to be seen. It had been expected that the ship would be safe for the winter, so the bales of fur were still aboard her, as were the belongings of many of the crew.

One week later Ollie Morris, a trapper from Barrow, and two Eskimos traveling with him by dogsled, reported that *Baychimo* had been located some eighteen miles south of Point Barrow and five miles out from the shore, but still standing. They were able to salvage a few bales of furs before leaving. Captain Cornwall and some of the crew traveled by dog team to see the ship, but it was still drifting and too far out to board. Once again he notified his superiors at the Hudson's Bay Company that Baychimo was unsalvageable and would no doubt sink.

It was mid-February before the marooned men on the shore near Wainwright could be flown out and then travel by train and steamship to Vancouver. They arrived there on March 8, 1932, eight months, almost to the day, from when they had left.

However, even after her final crew had gone on to their respective homes, *Baychimo* was still afloat! That March, Leslie Melvin, a trapper traveling by dogsled was able to board her and "salvage" some of Captain Cornwall's liquor, and a group of Eskimos was also able to approach and board her for a few hours.

Again, in August of the same year, the ship was sighted about seven miles from Wainwright. Several men went out to see if she could be salvaged, but unable to accomplish that, they removed dishes, guns, cameras, clothing, and even a lifeboat. Also in August, it was reported that a group of twenty to thirty Eskimos kayaked out to the ship and then were trapped there for ten days by a storm.

Rumors continued to abound that *Baychimo* carried a fortune in furs, and there were numerous reports of sightings throughout the winter months.

Then, on August 11, 1933, the little schooner *Trader*, with Isobel and its three-man crew aboard, dropped anchor in Wainwright. With the tale of the phantom ship still in her mind, Isobel was excited when Dick Hall and two Eskimos greeted them with "*Baychimo's* out there in the ice, twelve miles off shore! Can you get to her, boys?" *Trader* took them aboard and struck out through the ice floes. After several hours of careful maneuvering, they made it out to the drifting ship and boarded her. Although there had been a number of pillagers before them, there was much left amidst the already rifled but interesting contents. In the damp, drafty hold they found innumerable items, among which were sacks of mineral ore, caribou skins, a pair of handcuffs, a rusty typewriter, writing paper, a complete edition of *Times History of the Great War,* and even ledgers from the Hudson's Bay Company.

The Eskimos gathered mattresses and swivel chairs, while the crew of the *Trader* managed to secure the deck compass and one of the four repeaters of the gyrocompass. Isobel was disappointed not to find any Native artifacts, which she had heard were aboard. After all the desired items had been removed to the little schooner, it made its heavy-laden way back to shore.

The next day the Eskimos took two of their umiaks and made another, more dangerous journey across the ice and recovered a small whaleboat, along with cartons of Sunlight Soap, tins of Brasso, and a bucket of mixed pickles.

The next morning the ghost ship had again drifted across the ice and out of sight.

The little *Trader* had spent a good weather day on its *Baychimo* adventure, and was not able to get out from Wainwright for five more days, and what should have been a short few days' trip to Barrow was not accomplished until the first week in September. On their first two mornings they could just see

Baychimo, traveling almost out of sight on the horizon headed northeast. After that, she vanished again into the mist.

There have been many reported sightings, both documented and undocumented, of the "Ghost Ship of the Arctic" subsequent to the *Trader's* vision of it disappearing over the horizon in 1933.

In July of 1934 a crew from a small schooner reported finding her several miles from the northern coast of Alaska and boarding her.

In September of 1935 she was sighted close enough to the northwest coast of Alaska that she was at risk of being grounded, although still stuck in ice. But again the winds and currents sent her out of sight away from land.

Over the years Eskimo hunters and kayakers reported seeing *Baychimo* drifting around the seas.

In 1962 a group of kayaking hunters spotted her off the north Alaska coast. Although she was rusted and far off on the horizon, they could clearly read her name, *Baychimo,* on her bow. By the time they reached Barrow with their hunted bounty and told their story, the ship had once more disappeared.

The last recorded sighting of the phantom ship was in 1969, thirty-eight years after she was originally trapped in the ice. Some Eskimos among the crew of the US tanker *Manhattan* reported seeing *Baychimo* still trapped in an ice floe drifting between Icy Cape and Point Barrow.

Where is she now?

In all likelihood *Baychimo* is at the bottom of some arctic water, crushed to smithereens by the force of the flowing polar

PHOTO BY ISOBEL WYLIE HUTCHISON. COURTESY OF
ROYAL SCOTTISH GEOGRAPHICAL SOCIETY

The little *Trader* anchored to an ice floe beside the *Baychimo*

ice. But who's to say if some gray, misty morning she might once again loom out of the fog, just close enough to entice the observer to approach but not close enough to be caught?

Isobel Hutchison penned a poem, including these verses, after watching *Baychimo* disappear in the mist:

> *Fast frozen in the solid pack*
> *She rides the sheeted tide*
> *And follows on an unknown track*
> *Steered by a secret Guide.*

> *Ride On! Ride Out! We meet no more,*
> *Sad captive of the wave,*
> *Thy bourne some far forgotten shore,*
> *The polar night thy grave.*

CHAPTER 3

Ghostly Rescues

S tories and myths about ghosts, spirits, and other unknown entities are everywhere in Alaska. Ghosts have been rumored to appear just in time to offer assistance or, at the very least, encouragement, to those in most need. Sometimes the ghostly apparitions are witnessed by several people, but often, the only raconteur is a single seldom-believed individual!

One of the oft-told stories about help from an unknown source concerns the last voyage of the sidewheeler steamship *Eliza Anderson.*

On November 27, 1858, the *Eliza Anderson* was launched on her trial run for the Columbia River Steam Navigation Company. She was sold to a consortium that included Tom Wright and his two brothers, who operated several steamboats in the Pacific Northwest. A year later, Tom Wright, who became a legendary steamboatman in the area, took over as her captain, a position that he held for many years. *Eliza Anderson* served on the Olympia, Washington, to Victoria, British Columbia, mail route for almost fifteen years, and then was retired to Olympia. However, when the Cassiar Gold Rush began in the early 1870s, she was again put in service, carrying miners up the Inland Passage to Wrangell, Alaska, where they started the trek over the mountains to the Cassiar gold fields in British Columbia. By 1877 the *Eliza Anderson* had been retired again to Seattle and sank where she was moored.

Just five years later, Captain Wright raised his dear old steamship, pumped her out and put her to work on yet another route. Unfortunately by that time she could no longer compete against the newer, faster vessels, so Captain Wright was forced to sell her and the *Eliza Anderson* was eventually tied up on the Duwamish River in Washington State, where she was operated as a roadhouse and gambling hall.

Then came the discovery of gold in the Klondike, and the old side-wheeler's legendary story began.

Thousands of gold-seekers poured into Seattle, eager to find passage north to the country where they would seek their fortunes. These hordes of would-be millionaires were full of enthusiasm and willing to book passage on anything that would float. So all sorts of vessels were pulled out from wherever they had been left to waste away and forced back into service.

Sure enough, the *Eliza Anderson* was retrieved from her riverside docking, overhauled, and put back in the water on July 31, 1897, with Captain Thomas Powers in charge. Ten days later she joined a flotilla of four other vessels bound for Alaska. The grouping consisted of a steam tug, the *Richard Holyoke,* which towed behind it three other crafts, the sternwheeler *W. K. Merwin*, the old Russian side-wheeler *Politofsky*, and the yachting schooner *William J. Bryant.*

Many of the ships bound for the gold fields headed to Skagway, at the top of the Inland Passage. From there the gold-rushers would hike up the Chilkoot Trail, cross Lake Bennett and, eventually, travel on to Dawson, in the Yukon Territory. The *Eliza Anderson* and her entourage, however, were taking the route to St. Michael, a port on the western coast of Alaska, just south of Nome. From there the passengers would board the smaller steamboat, *Merwin,* for the trip up the Yukon River to the gold-fields. The *Merwin*, in fact, was boarded up, and parts of it were stored on the craft itself for the towing to St. Michael. Despite that, sixteen passengers agreed to book passage on it!

There was much speculation about the safety of the group of vessels heading north with the *Eliza Anderson.* The little flotilla of five was dubbed by some as "floating coffins." Nevertheless, off to the north they sailed.

The voyage was an accident waiting to happen from the very beginning. The company had way oversold the tickets, so passengers were vying with one another for space. Some counts say as many as 120 passengers were aboard. Others report a total of only forty. But however many there were, they had limited space.

The first mishap to befall the *Eliza Anderson* was the discovery that she had left port without some important equipment, most notably a navigational compass! The next occurred when they stopped at Connox, British Columbia. The inexperienced crew loading supplies somehow caused the steamship to veer into another vessel anchored nearby, damaging one of the paddlewheel guards. By the time the fleet finally reached Kodiak, five passengers disembarked, convinced that the ship would sink before it reached St. Michael, which was still quite a distance away. Regardless, the crew loaded in more coal, and the *Eliza Anderson* continued her ill-fated journey.

Shortly after leaving Kodiak the group of ships ran into one of the worst storms to hit the Gulf of Alaska. As the waves grew higher and the wind more fierce, the towline to the *Merwin* snapped, leaving it tossed about with the sixteen passengers holding on for dear life! With great difficulty and after several hours, it was finally reattached to the *Holyoke,* but by that time the *Holyoke* and the three ships she was towing had become separated from the *Eliza Anderson.* They were able to make their way to Dutch Harbor, and they reported the *Anderson* missing. The revenue cutter *Corwin* was sent out to search for her.

Meanwhile, the missing side-wheeler was having a terrible time. As the old vessel was knocked about by the thirty-foot waves, some of the welded seams cracked and she began to take on water. It also appeared that the crew had not loaded all of the sacks of coal that had been stacked on the dock in Kodiak and their coal supply was running out. As the fuel supply dwindled, the passengers and crew began ripping up furniture and storage boxes and anything else flammable to toss into the furnace, and they stuffed any kind of filling they could find into the widening cracks in the hull.

The storm had blown the *Eliza Anderson* badly off course, so that Captain Powers was not at all certain where they were, but he thought they were about thirty miles offshore from someplace on the Alaska Peninsula, still about 250 miles from Dutch Harbor. He knew that they did not have enough fuel to get to the port, but hoped they could reach the shore. As the storm reached the height of its intensity, Captain Powers ordered the lifeboats to be stocked with supplies, although he had little hope that they would be able to stay afloat in the rough waters. Passengers were writing notes and stuffing them into bottles to be tossed overboard in hopes that loved ones would someday know what had become of them.

On the verge of giving the order to abandon ship, Captain Powers stood on the bridge grasping the wheel, wondering if they could make the shore on the small amount of fuel remaining. Suddenly, out of the storm, a tall, ghostly figure with a long flowing beard and wearing full oilskin regalia strode into the wheelhouse and forcibly took over the helm. Seemingly fully aware of the plight of the ship, the figure pointed toward the shore.

"Thin Point," he shouted. He held tightly to the wheel and brought the vessel under control as the storm began to abate. The pale stranger headed toward a cove on Cold Bay, and there, slightly protected from the waves, the *Eliza Anderson* was able to drop anchor near the beach. As her paddlewheels ground to

UNIVERSITY OF WASHINGTON LIBRARIES, SPECIAL COLLECTIONS, UW7737, TRANSPORTATION COLLECTION

The *Eliza Anderson* in her final resting place in Dutch Harbor on Unalaska Island, Alaska, circa 1897

a stop, the passengers and crew drew deep sighs of relief. The storm slackened, and the travelers were able to see that the beach held the skeleton of an old abandoned cannery. Amazingly, there, protected under the wrecked roof, were seventy-five tons of coal! That would be more than enough to get them through to Dutch Harbor.

Captain Powers searched for the ghostly helmsman who had brought them safely through the storm and to their salvation, but he had disappeared as fleetingly as he had arrived.

The crew loaded the coal onto the side-wheeler while the passengers did what they could to repair the cracks enough to undertake the remainder of the trip to Dutch Harbor.

As the pathetic *Eliza Anderson* limped into the Unalaska port, she suffered one last embarrassment. As she approached the docks, the vessel swiveled into them with a splintering crash. At the same time, a pipe in the boiler room broke, spouting scalding steam everywhere. Although Captain Powers wanted to sail on to St. Michael, twenty-eight of the passengers on the *Eliza Anderson* were so distraught that they immediately sought passage on a return trip to Seattle, and the rest of them looked for other transportation to the mouth of the Yukon River. Also, the revenue officers deemed the *Anderson* unfit for further duty, so she lay at anchor there until another storm a month later dashed her into the rocks and ended her sad story.

But what about the ghostly stranger who appeared out of nowhere to steer the troubled side-wheeler to safety, and then disappeared into nowhere again? Two years after her demise, an article in the *Seattle Post-Intelligencer* quoted an old sailor who had been on the ill-fated voyage and believed that the stranger was a ghost.

"It was Tom Wright's spirit," he said. "The old man was her captain for many years, and he loved the *Anderson.* He knew of her peril and came to guide her to a port of safety." Then, "Captain Tom's spirit saw our danger and brought us safely to land."

That explanation made the rounds of the seagoing community and was believed for many years by those who were superstitious. There was one small problem with the theory, however. It seems that Captain Tom Wright was very much alive at the time of the ghostly rescue. He died eight years later!

So who was the ghostly figure that saved the ship? In the early 1950s this story surfaced from a crewman of the *Corwin* that had searched for the *Eliza Anderson* out of Dutch Harbor. It seems that there were two brothers who had operated the cannery where the *Anderson* found safety. One of them had stowed away on it in Kodiak, hoping to persuade a relative in Dutch Harbor to lend them money. When the ship was apparently lost, he came into the wheelhouse and steered it into the cove near the cannery. He then hid again until they reached Dutch Harbor. Many yarn tellers prefer the ghostly stranger version.

Another spirited rescue story involves a ghost who wasn't a stranger at all. The *Nome Nugget* published a story on September 7, 1901, about H. O. Blankenship, one of the first miners to find gold on Candle Creek, off of Kotzebue Sound.

Earlier that year, a psychic had given Mr. Blankenship the names of three spots where he should look for gold. On June 9 he started out from Nome in a small boat, headed north around the Seward Peninsula. He traveled with a companion as far as Cape Prince of Wales, but from there went on alone. There was still heavy ice in the Bering Strait, and he was carried on the currents quite a way out to sea. He realized that he was in the Arctic Ocean when he saw a whale near his boat! He knew he would reach land if he traveled east, so he began to row, as there was little wind for the sail. For eight days he traveled through the perilous ice. He was directed through the ice by a figure that he recognized as his deceased father-in-law.

"I could see him plainly, as I saw him in life. He would sit in the bow of the boat, and by a motion of the hand would indicate how I should steer."

Twice during the eight days Blankenship was able to tie up to an ice floe and sleep briefly. Finally he reached land and slept for sixteen hours before traveling on to the Kiwalik River and Candle Creek on July 26. He prospected there, found gold, staked three claims, and left the creek on August 23.

The same story is told in a book, *Nome and Seward Peninsula: history, description, biographies and stories,* by Edward Harrison, published in 1905. Harrison writes, "The discovery of gold on Candle Creek furnishes a first-class spook story."

It is obviously the same storyteller mentioned in the Nome newspaper, although Harrison identifies him as G. W. Blankenship. There are other slight discrepancies in the two tales. Harrison doesn't mention the psychic, or a companion for the first leg of the trip. Also, he places the "spook guide" in the stern of the boat, motioning with his hands to direct which way Blankenship should row. But the important part of the story is there, that he "recognized the spirit as the shade of his deceased father-in-law." Additionally, in this version Blankenship is not only guided where to land, but also directed to Candle Creek and the spots to find gold.

Harrison ends his tale, "This is the story that Blankenship told me. The reader may accept it or reject it, according to his point of view of things that are 'not dreamed of in our philosophy.'"

Another specter appeared to give unexpected assistance to a lone mariner a half century later. Bart Jacobsen had an encounter with an unknown ghostly rescuer in August of 1957. Bart was a herring fisherman, working out of Halibut Cove in Kachemak Bay with his boat, the *Midnight Sun.*

One day he was fishing in the upper Cook Inlet and had started home with his catch. He knew there was a storm coming and hoped to reach the safety of the bay before it caught up with him. But soon the swells became deeper, reaching up to eight feet. The skiff, which he towed behind his boat to carry gear, began taking on water. Caught in the rip tide, the skiff was quickly being swamped. Bart knew that he would have to bail the water out of it. He pulled the skiff in and secured it to the side of the boat, climbed aboard it, and began to bail. He scooped and bailed, scooped and bailed. Suddenly the line to the boat tightened, pulling the little skiff sideways. Bart realized that the engine had quit and the line was wrapped around the wheel, pulling the skiff up and over toward the boat deck. He jumped back aboard and began trying to loosen the line from the stern of the boat. He struggled fruitlessly until he knew that the only option was to release the skiff. With a kitchen knife he cut the line and watched helplessly as the skiff was tossed away on ever deepening swells.

Without the weight of the skiff, the *Midnight Sun* began twirling and pitching, spinning around on the waves.

"Throw out the net," came a voice out of the wind.

Bart turned and saw a man standing on the deck. Instinctively, he knew the man's name was John.

"Throw out the net and make a sea anchor," said John.

"I know that. Why didn't I think of it?" Bart answered.

"You better eat something," said John.

Bart crawled to the cabin and got an orange. He peeled it, pulled it in half, and set one half down for John. But as he began to eat the orange, he realized that John was not real, so he ate both halves himself!

Feeling refreshed, Bart went back to the task of cutting the line away from the wheel so that it would not become tangled in the propeller. Leaning over the stern he sawed and sawed, with the boat plunging down into the wave trough then up again to the top. Finally he felt the knife blade touch metal, and the line loosened. Bart made his way again to the cabin, where he grasped the wheel and found it moving free. He turned the key in the ignition, and the engine coughed to a start. The storm was beginning to abate. As Bart noted that he was still out in the inlet, just off of Augustine, he set his course toward Kachemak Bay.

Some time later, well inside the safety of the bay, Bart started to drop anchor.

"Don't stop now," insisted John, suddenly appearing again in the cabin.

"But I want to sleep," Bart answered.

"No, don't sleep now. Go home."

"But I need sleep!" Bart argued.

"No, go home!" John repeated. "Then you can sleep all you want."

So an exhausted Bart took the *Midnight Sun* all the way to Halibut Cove before he tied her to the mooring and dragged himself home.

After hearing Bart's tale, his neighbors had some questions. How did Bart know it was "John" and not some other name? Did he look like someone Bart knew? Did he really not know who John was?

"I don't know how I knew!" Bart replied. "But he sure was there. He sure saved me, but he sure was bossy!"

So where do they come from, these ghostly rescuers? Maybe they are long deceased sailors, who keep watch o'er the waters where they once plied their trades. Maybe they are figments in the imagination of weary seamen struggling against all odds, searching for help from above.

CHAPTER 4

The Hairy Man

Storytelling is an integral part of Alaskan culture, and stories about the Hairy Man abound throughout the state. He is known by various names, such as Arulataq, Ahoolahuk, Kushtaka, Urayuli, Nant'ina, Nantiinaq, or Get'qun, depending on which part of the state is referenced. Sometimes, he is just "Hairy Man." But all of the stories describe him in a similar way.

Generally, the creature is described as tall, seven feet or more. He is covered with long brown or black or red hair, and has a humanlike face. His arms are long, reaching down to his knees. He has long legs and travels with giant strides, covering ground more rapidly than any man could move. He leaps over rocks and pushes large alders out of his way. A horrible smell is reputed to surround him, and he emits "unearthly" screams.

Alaska Native people have handed down stories about this creature for generations. The general understanding among them is that he keeps careful watch, and will make himself known whenever he deems it necessary, especially in times when they are

The definitive Alaska Hairy Man; note "Alaska Hand" (see introduction)

ARTIST CREDIT: TAYLOR MEDLEY, SCISSORKICK!

intruding upon his habitat. However, as Alaska becomes more populated and more outsiders come to visit, it is not just Native people who have come forward with stories about unexplained sightings and happenings.

There have been sightings of these unexplained creatures from almost every part of Alaska. But sightings seem to be more prevalent in some South Central and Southeastern communities. Southwest of Anchorage is the Kenai Peninsula. On the very southwestern part of that peninsula is an area, across Kachemak Bay from Homer, which has fostered many Hairy Man sightings.

In 2009 Naomi Klouda, a reporter with the *Homer Tribune,* had an opportunity to interview Malania Helen Kehl, the eldest resident of Nanwalek at the time. Nanwalek is a small village at the very southernmost tip of the Kenai Peninsula. It was once a Russian trading post and boasts a Russian Orthodox church that is a National Historic Site. The current residents are mostly mixed Russian and Alutiiq. They speak an Eskimo dialect similar to Yup'ik.

Malania Kehl was born in Port Chatham in 1934. It was a small village nestled up in a protected bay just around the shore to the southeast of where Nanwalek is now. But when she was still a baby, her parents packed up and moved everything they had to Nanwalek, or, English Bay, as it was then known. It seems that for some time the villagers in Port Chatham had been "bothered" by a nantiinaq, or "big hairy creature." Finally, after years of terror, the villagers "left our houses and the school, and started all new here." Although Malania says that after her family moved to Nanwalek the nantiinaq didn't bother them again, there are other residents in the village who still have stories to tell about the creature.

In January of 2010, Brad Josephs and a friend spent two weeks in Nanwalek, interviewing the elders about the nantiinaq. Josephs, who lives in Homer, is a naturalist interpreter with a degree in wildlife biology from the University of Alaska, Fairbanks. He leads bear-viewing expeditions in Katmai National Park and is a recognized authority on bear behavior.

Josephs and his friend found that there is a general understanding among the villagers that the creature exists in various forms. The creature can be in animal form similar to a bear although walking on two feet but also is recognized as a spirit. Sometimes the spirit is angry and dangerous, and that is when more sightings of the animal form appear. The villagers refer to "nantiinaq" but also call it the "Hairy Man." There is some feeling that when a village is having problems, or interfering with the environment, then the creature, or creatures, come around to let the villagers know they are not happy. After the villages of Port Chatham, and later Portlock, were abandoned by the 1950s because of unexplained happenings, there were very few encounters for the next several years. However, recently the sightings have increased.

There is a chain of lakes up a river from Nanwalek. According to Brad, the natives believe the first lake is haunted and not a safe place. A few years ago a forestry crew on a fire management program was spending the night there when they heard wild screaming and trees crashing down. They took off back into town, and several of the natives went back up together to investigate. They reported screams and ape-like yells that were definitely not bear noises but found no source for the disturbances.

Another time a family was fishing on that same river when the father saw a large, hairy creature, standing about seven feet tall at the edge of the water. He made eye contact with it, and it disappeared into the trees. He sent his wife and two daughters back into town and got his gun, but the Hairy Man was gone.

Brad has heard other tales of the Hairy Man over the years, and has, himself, had two experiences with "it." His first encounter happened when he was guiding a small group of four tourists on a bear-viewing trip along a secluded coast of Katmai National Park. Near dark, he was washing dishes when he heard an earsplitting and unearthly scream from up in the valley. He was so startled that he dropped a plate! He described the scream as sounding like "howler monkeys," only deeper and longer.

The second encounter occurred around Portlock. During a hiking trip about ten years ago, Josephs was looking at some deserted buildings when he was especially impressed by a large cabin. He then went back a few years later to film in the area. He wanted to spend the night in the cabin, but a strange feeling discouraged him. The next day he returned, and there was an old shoe situated prominently in the middle of the cabin's threshold.

That incident had some similarity to a story he had heard from a long-time park ranger who, with another ranger, was crossing between Katmai and Bristol Bay when a storm hit. They were inside their tent when they heard an ungodly roar and the sound of a creature nearby. The other ranger said, "It's the Hairy Man, and he's not happy we're here!" The next morning there was a tennis shoe outside the door of the tent. They immediately retraced their steps and waited for a plane to come and get them.

Ed Schlief, owner of Alaska Bowhunting Supply in Anchorage, also tells a riveting story. In 1990, working as a paramedic, he and his partner were transporting an elderly man to the Native Hospital in Anchorage. During their conversation, Ed discovered that the man was an Aleut from Port Graham, so he mentioned that he and some friends had once been caught in a storm at the upper end of Dogfish Bay, near Port Graham. The old man immediately sat up and grabbed Ed's shirt and asked, "Did it bother you?"

Ed continued the story; "Well, with that the hair just stood up on the back of my head. I said, 'Yes!' 'Did you see it?' was his next question. I said, 'No, did you see it?' He said, 'No, but my brother seen it! It chased him!' This old Aleut and I were talking about the same thing, but we never used the word Bigfoot or Hairy Man or anything like that. But we both knew what we were talking about."

Ed's encounter occurred in August of 1973 when he and two friends were bowhunting in that southwestern tip of the

Kenai Peninsula. A storm had forced them up into Dogfish Bay. They beached their skiff and set up a canvas tent. After dinner of salmon and cleaning the pots to discourage bears, they "turned in." At 2:00 a.m. Ed was awakened by one of his friends. "Listen!" They woke the third member of the party, and they all heard it. There was someone circling the tent, walking slowly and deliberately, and then it stopped. The next morning there was nothing, no footprints. They continued their hunt with no mention of the footsteps.

That night the weather had kept them in the same spot. About 2:30 a.m. they heard the footsteps, not ten feet from the tent, begin their circling again. They had flashlights at the ready, but by the time they were courageous enough to shine the flashlight outside, they saw nothing, no tracks. The boys decided that if it came back the third night they would "come out of the tent shooting."

But the third night they heard no footsteps, and the next day the weather cleared and they "got the heck out of there."

Another story comes from Greg Christian who lives on Tutka Island in Little Tutka Bay, directly south from Homer across Kachemak Bay. He has had two encounters with the Hairy Man.

In the early 1990s Greg and some friends were hunting moose near the deserted town of Port Chatham. He and a couple of others hiked up along a creek, through grass that was about four feet tall. They came to an area where the grass had been systematically patted down, to make two rectangular "rooms." They had never seen any kind of animal that made that kind of a "nest," but it was definitely a purposeful design. The other two hunters returned to the boat, but Greg continued up the creek to an open area surrounded by spruce trees. Spotting no moose, he started back, and as he came around a corner, he felt as if he were being watched. He stopped, looked back, and heard a bone-chilling scream, high-pitched and guttural. He returned rapidly down the creek to his friends, who razzed him mercilessly about his story.

Several years later in 2004, Greg was building a house in Little Tutka, a small bay across Kachemak from Homer. One Friday afternoon in the fall, he and another worker left to spend the weekend in Homer. As they passed Kayak Beach between Sadie Cove and Tutka, their boat was about seventy-five yards off shore and Greg was on the shore side. He always watched the shore, and suddenly he saw a very tall creature, just as he had heard the Hairy Man described. It had dark hair all over, walked erect with very large strides and swung its long arms along as it walked, and its head was turned left looking at the boat. Greg actually made eye contact with the creature, but by the time he alerted the other man in the boat the Hairy Man had disappeared from the beach.

When he returned to Little Tutka on Monday morning, he met up with three of his friends and told them what he had seen. He was expecting the usual razzing and was surprised when they just looked at each other. It seems that while they were hunting on Saturday morning just a mile or so from Kayak Beach, they had come across some droppings, or scat, that they could not identify as being from any animal with which they were familiar, and they had hunted in the area for many years. Coincidentally, one of the men was Randy Arsunalt, who had been one of Greg's "razzers" during his first encounter.

In the late 1970s, Ted Gerken and his business partner put all of their money in a "frontier fishing lodge" on Lake Iliamna. The lake is the largest one in Alaska and is located at the north end of the Alaska Peninsula about one hundred miles west of Kachemak Bay. The Athabascan natives in the area have many stories to tell about the Hairy Man, or Big Man, or Get'qun, as they refer to him. One story tells of a creature captured with a net and put into a shed, but it managed to escape. Another tells of whole families of creatures that would occasionally visit.

Ted relates his encounter with Big Man in his book about their lodge, *Gamble at Iliamna*. His tale starts with Jim Coffee, a local maintenance man, who reported that as he was driving to the airport late one January night, he saw a nine-foot-tall creature on the road in front of him. As it took off into the bushes, Jim took three or four shots at it with his .357 Magnum pistol. The next day Ted and his wife, Mary, drove out to the spot where Jim had seen the creature. Ted was skeptical, even though they found large tracks in the light snow by the side of the road. The tracks were twenty-two inches long, twelve inches across three toes, and six inches at the heel. The length between strides was measured at three feet. Still, Ted thought they could have been made as a prank with plywood snowshoes. But then the tracks left the road.

Ted wrote, "I could clearly see each footprint dug into the side of the snow berm, with the uphill side of the track definitely cut deeper into the hill than the downhill side. I didn't believe a man with plywood snowshoes could make such tracks on a hill. And they definitely weren't the tracks of either a bear or moose, the largest animals known in this area."

Adding to the intrigue, that same night the cook at the lodge had been visiting her neighbor, a few hundred feet from her house. When she left to return home with her toddler son, she felt that she was being watched. After giving her son a bath and putting him to bed, she opened the entryway intending to throw out the water. She again felt she was being watched and smelled a nauseating rotten animal smell, so she slammed and locked the door. In the morning she saw the biggest footprints she had ever seen. They led around to her window, then across to her neighbor's yard, where two sheets and pillowcases were missing from the laundry line. Speculation was that Jim had wounded the creature and it stole the linens to bind up its wounds.

It was also reported that when Jim and another man went back to see if there was any "evidence" of the creature, they found drops of what looked like transmission fluid that they surmised might be blood.

Another part of Alaska that seems to harbor vast numbers of "Kushtaka" stories and sightings is the Southeast, especially around Saxman and Ketchikan and north to Juneau and even Haines.

J. Robert Alley, in his book, *Raincoast Sasquatch*, has related thousands of reports of encounters with the creatures. They range from brief glimpses along the sides of the road, to being in a car that was picked up from the rear and shaken for several minutes, to having logs or huge snowballs hurled at people, or being chased by screaming creatures. There is even a story from 1924 of a prospector being kidnapped and held for several days by a family of "Sasquatches," a term generally used to describe the "Hairy Man" reported to inhabit the Pacific Northwest of the United States and British Columbia.

Alley, who lives in Ketchikan, has been a researcher with the North American Bigfoot Search team since 1974. He has measured huge footprints, been shown plaster casts of huge footprints, listened to recordings of ape-like vocalizations, collected bits of unidentifiable hair, observed large nests both on the ground and in trees in remote and uninhabited wilderness and listened to endless first-person stories of meetings with the Hairy Man. He has heard countless descriptions of individual creatures, of pairs, of family groups, or of mothers and infants. Sometimes the creatures are perceived to be hostile, many times only curious, even friendly. Seemingly conclusive evidence indicates that somewhere out there in the wilderness there dwells a class of large primates that is living quite successfully in the shadow of civilization.

But far from giving answers, the evidence seems only to produce more questions. How many of these creatures actually exist? How do they remain so elusive? Do they live in families? What do they do in the winter? What do they eat?

Still, the scientific community remains unconvinced, due to the lack of an actual specimen, either alive or dead. But ask any Nanwalek elder, or Brad Josephs, or Ed Schlief, or Greg Christian and his friend, Randy, or any one of the first-person-reporters to J. Robert Alley. They all know that the Hairy Man is alive and well in the wilderness.

CHAPTER 5

What Is under the Water?

From early times, Alaska Native people who live in the area around Lake Iliamna have been leery of a huge unknown creature residing in the water there. The Aleut name for it is "Jig-ik-nak," although more commonly now referred to as "Illie." The name of the lake, "Iliamna," is said to mean in the Aleut language, something like "a great blackfish inhabits this lake and bites holes in the bidarkas of people who have strayed from the ways of the tribe." Supposedly, this creature attacks and sinks boats with red hulls, leaves people who see it cursed, and has even eaten people.

Lake Iliamna is the largest lake in Alaska. It is seventy-seven miles long and twenty-two miles wide and almost a thousand feet deep at its deepest point. It is connected to Bristol Bay by the Kvichak River, which flows out from its southwest end. There is one gravel utility road that goes from Pile Bay at the northeast end of the lake across to Williamsport, which is a tiny town on Iliamna Bay on Cook Inlet. The road is not intended for general use, so the only access to Lake Iliamna is by boat up the river from Bristol Bay or by air. Roughly fifteen miles of road connect the villages of Newhalen, Iliamna, and Seversens, and up the Newhalen River to tiny Gaging Station and Lake Clark. Iliamna, Kokhanok, Pedro Bay, and Igiugig all have landing strips. Float-planes and lake boats service the remaining small settlements and tourist lodges sprinkled sparsely around the perimeter.

Because the lake is so large, and has been so lightly popu-lated in the past, it is not unlikely that there could be denizens of the water that are not often seen by human eyes. But as the lake gathered a reputation for being a great sport fishing area, more and more people were attracted to it. As more small aircraft flew over the lake, bringing supplies to the remote fishing and hunt-ing lodges as well as the Native villages, more eyes were able to observe large unidentifiable swimming creatures. In the 1940s rumors started coming in from flyers reporting monsters in the lake. The descriptions were similar to the ones from Native sto-ries: long, thin animals that swam like fish and were up to thirty feet long! The big fish, whatever they were, began to be referred to affectionately as the "Illies."

Leon Alsworth, a missionary and bush pilot known to every-one as Babe, lived on Hardenburg Bay in Lake Clark. In 1942 he and a fisherman friend, Bill Hammersly, were flying over a shal-low part of Lake Iliamna and saw several large animals swimming below them. Babe described the creatures as having fishlike tails and elongated bodies with broad, blunt heads. They were well over ten feet long and were the color of dull aluminum. Although Babe flew over the lake more than a hundred times in the next half century, he never saw the big fish again. Bill Hammersly remained fascinated by the monster fish and reportedly participated in an attempt to catch one using a seaplane as a dock, a hook of a foot-long rod with a hunk of moose as bait, and several hundred feet of stainless-steel aircraft cable as a line with a fifty-five-foot oil drum as a bobber. The four men in on this attempt claimed that something "big" was hooked but that it broke the cable and "got away."

Larry Rost was a US Coast and Geodetic Survey pilot. In 1945 he was flying over Lake Iliamna and sighted a giant fish that was more than twenty feet long, and he also described it as the color of dull aluminum. Almost twenty years later an unidentified wildlife biologist also reported seeing a twenty-foot-long creature in the lake.

Tom Slick was a Texas oil tycoon and philanthropist who graduated from Yale, a Phi Beta Kappa with a biology degree, and did graduate work at both Harvard and MIT. He used his inherited millions to fund scientific research, oil drilling, cattle breeding, exploration, and collections of modern art. He also established several research organizations including the Institute of Inventive Research, the Mind Science Foundation, and the Human Progress Foundation.

Slick became intrigued with cryptozoology, which is defined as "the search for and study of animals whose existence or survival is disputed, such as the Loch Ness Monster or the Yeti." He organized and participated in a search for the Yeti, the "Abominable Snowman," and then turned his attention to Alaska.

In 1959 Slick spent thousands of dollars in search of the strange creatures in Lake Iliamna. He hired Babe Alsworth to fly him over the lake several times, and even hired a helicopter that hovered over the spot where Babe had seen the big fish. Slick was still hoping to find the elusive monster when he was killed in an airplane crash in 1962.

Tim LaPorte has operated Iliamna Air Taxi Service since 1977. That year he was flying with two passengers over the northeast end of the lake near San Pedro. All three of the men watched as a very large creature that was resting in the water with its back just barely above the surface made a huge arched splash and dove straight down as the plane approached. They described the animal as twelve to fourteen feet in length and dark gray or brown in color.

Then again in 1987, a large unidentifiable creature was spotted. Three women were fishing in the lake about five miles from the village of Pedro Bay, and came within one hundred feet of the creature. One of the women described it as being shaped more like a whale, with a white stripe along a fin on its back. She was quoted as saying, "It made an almost complete circle around us."

Back on shore, the owner of the Rainbow Bay Resort, Jerry Pippen, took to the air as soon as he heard about the sighting. He spotted a large ripple in the lake, but no creature. However, the next day he saw "a really huge seal. This seal was squirting water six to eight feet in the air."

So, the question remains: Is there a solution to the mystery of the monster fish inhabiting the waters of Iliamna?

And the answer is: There doesn't appear to be any solution that provides indisputable physical proof, but there are a number of logical explanations waiting for verification.

At least some of the dark brown or black creatures described might be big seals. Although freshwater seals are considered rare, they are definitely present in Lake Iliamna, one of only five populations in northern hemisphere lakes. The exact species of seal is not certain, but they are thought to be harbor seals or possibly spotted seals. Some of the seals are in the lake year-round. Some might travel to Bristol Bay down the Kvichak River, but actual seal migrations have not been recorded. There have been seals in the lake for a very long time, as Native people there have hunted them for many generations.

Recently Bruce Wright, a senior scientist at the Aleutian Pribilof Island Association, has suggested the Loch Ness Monster and the Lake Iliamna Big Fish might be sleeper sharks. He noted similarities in the descriptions of the sharks and the lake creatures and hopes to find more information by using underwater cameras in both Alaska and Scotland. Sleeper sharks can be twenty feet or longer and weigh up to four tons. But it is unclear at this point how long they might be able to survive in fresh water.

One generally accepted explanation is that the creatures are land-locked white sturgeons. The descriptions of these giant fish are very similar to those of the "Illies."

Could an ugly white sturgeon like this be the Big Fish in Iliamna?

PHOTO BY LARA CERRI © *TAMPA BAY TIMES*

According to the Pacific States Marine Fisheries Commission, white sturgeons are the largest freshwater fish in North America. They can weigh over 1,500 pounds and be twenty feet in length. They can live for over one hundred years. These huge fish don't have scales but have "scutes," which are bony plates that are arranged in two lines down their back, a line of them along each side, and one underneath, giving them a sort of armored appearance. In color they are gray, pale olive, or gray-brown, with fins of a dusky, opaque gray. Underneath they are white.

Sturgeons are bottom-feeders and spend most of their lives in bays, estuaries, and the brackish water at the mouths of wide rivers. They swim upstream to spawn, and the juveniles can remain in the freshwater rivers or lakes until maturity, which could be five to eleven years. They grow very slowly, and after twenty-five years might still be only ten feet long. In North America their range is from Ensenada, Mexico, to Cook Inlet, Alaska.

So it is possible that sometime in the last hundred years or so, sturgeons may have made their way up the Kvichak River and not been able to get back to Bristol Bay for some reason or another. There is a documented sturgeon catch in Bristol Bay, so that is in the realm of possibility. It has even been suggested that, since sturgeon have survived unchanged for millions of years, that they might have been trapped in the lake when the glaciers receded and have developed in isolation. Their slow rate of growth could account for the difference in lengths described. And their bottom-feeding habits could account for the rarity of the sightings.

At any rate, taking into consideration all of the different descriptions from all of the known sightings, it is logical to assume that the "Big Fish" of Iliamna are, indeed, sturgeons. But still, there is no physical proof of that premise being the final answer. And, what if they are not sturgeons?

Maybe they are "cryptids," one of the unidentified species studied by cryptozoologists.

Maybe they are Tizheruks. Those cryptids have mostly been reported around King Island or Nunivak Island in the Bering Sea but have also been reported in the Kuskokwim River, so maybe they made their way up the Kvichak to Lake Iliamna. But they don't really fit the descriptions of Illies. Tizheruks are up to fifteen feet long, and that is similar to Illie size. But unlike Illies, they have thick fur and short horns, three pairs of legs, and attack humans in kayaks. Probably the Illies are not Tizheruks.

For centuries there have been reports of gigantic sea creatures observed by sailing ships all over the world. In 1852 the whaling ship *Monongahela* came upon a huge creature flailing about in the waters of the Pacific, as if in great pain. First thinking it to be a whale that had been injured by harpoons from another ship, the Captain, Jason Seabury, sent his crew out in longboats to harvest it. Still thinking it to be a wounded whale, the sailors threw their harpoons. Amazingly, a beast, with a huge ten-foot-long head like nothing they had ever seen, rose out of the water, thrashing about and capsizing two of the boats. The *Monongahela* was able to pull alongside the overturned boats and rescue the sailors.

The next morning a massive dead beast floated up from the depths. It was longer than the one-hundred-foot-long ship itself, with a thick body fifty feet in diameter, of a brownish gray color. Its neck was ten feet around and the gigantic head was shaped like an alligator. It had ninety-four teeth that were curved backward like a snake's. Captain Seabury ordered the head to be cut off and put into a huge pickling vat, as proof of what they had seen.

Another ship, the *Rebecca Sims,* under a Captain Gavitt, pulled alongside. The *Monongahela* was on its way north to begin its whaling season in the Bering Sea, while the *Rebecca Sims* was on its way home to New England. Captain Seabury wrote out a detailed report of their encounter and sent it along with Captain Gavitt.

Presumably Captain Gavitt fulfilled his duty, as stories about the "Monongahela monster" appeared in several newspapers that year. But as for Captain Seabury, his ship, his crew, and the pickled monster head, nothing was ever heard of again. Several years later the ship's name board was found on the shore of Umnak Island in the Aleutians.

In 2009 fisherman Kelly Nash took some video of a strange creature swimming in Nushagak Bay in Alaska. The film was viewed by Dr. Paul Leblond, a noted academic known for his work in the field of ocean sciences. Dr. Leblond is a former director of the International Society of Cryptozoology and has written the defining work on *Cadborosaurus willsi,* a cryptid reportedly residing along the northern Pacific coasts of British Columbia and Alaska. After viewing the film, Dr. Leblond was quoted as saying, "That looks a lot like Cadborosaurus."

Nushagak Bay is adjacent to Kvichak Bay, where the river drains from Lake Illiamna. Presumably because of that, Jonathon and Andy Hillstrand, two brothers from Homer, Alaska, mounted a ludicrous but well-publicized search of the lake using similar large "fishing equipment" used by Bill Hammersly and his crew back in the 1940s.

Needless to say, they had no better luck than did those earlier searchers.

Loren Coleman is a well-known and respected American cryptozoologist. In 2009 he featured on his website a paper published by a British doctoral student and his two advisors. The basic premise of this paper was that there is such a vast volume of unexplored seas that it is not unexpected that more undiscovered creatures are living in them awaiting recognition. The authors pointed out that in just the past thirty years there had been several large marine animals discovered, such as the Lesser or Peruvian beaked whale, a giant filter-feeding shark known as the Megamouth, the Indonesian coelacanth, and the Omura's whale, a close relative of the Blue whale.

Bearing all this in mind, and applying that premise to Lake Iliamna, it is possible that since the lake is so large and impossible to see all at one time, that there may well be creatures swimming in it that have seldom, or even never, been seen by the human eye.

In the summer of 2011 the fossil of a large little-known seagoing reptile from the age of the dinosaurs was discovered near Kake in Southeast Alaska. It was identified as a thalaattosaur, which is Greek for "sea lizard."

Fossilized evidence has proven that there were many large previously unknown fish and seagoing reptiles swimming in Alaska's ancient waters.

Do the sightings of the Lake Iliamna Big Fish provide anecdotal evidence that something large and previously unknown is still swimming in Alaska's waters today?

In 1989 Louise Wasillie watched a large creature swimming beside her boat on Lake Iliamna.

"It's just a fish," she said.

CHAPTER 6

The "Little People" of the Arctic

In the spring of 2008 there was a fascinating story making its way around the Internet from the depths of rural Alaska. A hunter from Marshall, about sixty miles north of Bethel, had been out on his snowmobile hunting birds. He reportedly came across a small boy sitting by himself in the middle of a large marshy area. The child seemed dazed and disoriented and didn't know where his dad was or if he had been with other hunters. The hunter who found him asked some other nearby snowmobilers, but none of them had noticed the boy or knew how he got there. There were no footprints or tracks around him to indicate that anyone had driven him there. The boy was taken back to the village, where he told a strange story. He claimed that he had been taken inside of nearby Pilcher Mountain by ircenrraats, or "little beings." He told of meeting another child who had been taken into the mountain forty years ago. The ircenrraats then decided to let the boy go, and left him sitting where the hunter found him. He seemed to have lost some time and didn't remember when he had been taken.

Although most web readers of the story took it with a grain of salt, as just a story, there were others who firmly believed the tale.

There is a long history of belief in small, humanlike beings among the Inuit and Yup'ik Eskimo Native people of Alaska. The stories go back to the beginning of time when the small beings and people lived near each other.

In the 1880s a large collection of Yup'ik artifacts were amassed at the Berlin Ethnologisches Museum. More than a century later, a group of elders from Bethel traveled there to see the artifacts and discuss them with teachers from both countries. Ann Fienup-Riordan collected and edited their discussions for a book, *Things of Our Ancestors.* She also edited a book, *Wise Words of the Yup'ik People: We Talk to You Because We Love You,* from interviews with the Calista Elders Council in Southwest Alaska. These stories are retold primarily from her interviews.

One time a long time ago Little Man, Little Wife, and Little Boy visited a neighboring Inuit family. Little Boy was so small he wore a caribou ear for a parka. Little Boy wandered too close to a husky dog that was tied up nearby and was pounced on and eaten. Little Man grabbed the husky and ripped him apart with his bare hands. After that all the little people moved away from the village and lived underground. They became very shy to be seen by humans.

There are many names for these seldom seen little beings. In the northwest part of Alaska, the area from Nome to Barrow and along the North Slope, Inuit Eskimos know them as enukins, or ingnakalaurak. These are small, about three feet tall, mischievous creatures that are out and about mostly at night. They live in the old ways, wearing caribou skins and using bows and arrows. They are very strong, and one enukin can carry a whole caribou over his head while running. (That might explain why some bush pilots have claimed that they saw a caribou running on its side. One pilot also reported that he saw a caribou herd running, but when he flew down closer to look, it was a group of small people dressed in furs and carrying bows and arrows, running very fast.)

Sometimes enukins steal the caribou that a hunter has killed, but their mischief is not always bad.

One time a hunter was way out in the tundra, and his Honda ATV got stuck in the mud. He pushed and pulled to get it out but was finally too exhausted to keep trying. Suddenly the Honda came up in the air and bounced to solid ground, and he saw out of the corner of his eye a sort of a blur, running away. When someone is in trouble these little people come out of nowhere to help but then are gone in a flash.

The Yup'ik Eskimos, living more in the southwest part of Alaska from St. Michael to about Dillingham and inland, have many names for the little beings.

Ircenrraat, or tundra people, are about three feet tall. They are seen during berry season, and it is good luck to receive something from them. If a woman is given a basket, she will always find good berry bushes. If a hunter is given a knife, he will have good luck hunting all of his life.

Egassuayaq are shorter, only about one foot tall. It is bad luck to receive something from one of them. They will steal blackfish from the people's traps.

Paalraayak are "extraordinary creatures encountered in the mountainous regions," and can move about underground. Ircenrraat are also "extraordinary creatures" or "little people encountered in the wilderness." They also move about under the ground and are sometimes described as having elongated heads, with slitlike eyes or vertical eyes. Both of these creatures can appear in either animal or human form. They are sometimes seen but sometimes only heard.

One time a man and his wife were hunting squirrels near Assigy-ugpak, south of Togiak on Bristol Bay, not far from an area where, long ago, people had been told not to go. They saw a creature that looked like a land otter, and they had heard that paalraayak sometimes resembled land otters. The otter sank down into the ground when it walked. Then they realized that the sled they were pulling was sinking into the ground, which should still have been frozen from the winter. They sank farther and farther down, but then a person walked near them, and they were on top of the ground again. They began to sink once more, but as they got closer to their camp, the land otter disappeared under the ground, and then they were back on top of the ground and happy to be safe.

One time a man was paddling his kayak along the river when he noticed a village where people were busy going about their work and play. After he passed by the village, he looked back and saw several white foxes playing together. He realized that they were ircenrraat that had changed into human form as he paddled by them.

Sometimes people from a village are restricted during the time that they might be associated with birth, miscarriage, puberty, or death. Traditionally they abstain from certain practices during that time. They are also told not to go into the mountains because the ircenrraat will throw rocks at them.

One time some men were getting ready to go out and check their traps. One of the men was restricted, so the others told him not to kill an animal caught in his trap. But after the others had left, the restricted man checked his trap, and there was a fox trying to get away, so he killed it, even though he had been told not to do so. He started back to the village but heard voices shouting, "There is something in the water! Hit it!" The man fell down to his knees. "It just dove into the water!" He started to crawl. "You can see its wake on the water! Hit it!" He stood back up. "It came back up! Hit it!" Then he lay down on the ground and was very still. "We can't see the ripples anymore. He is gone. We have lost him." The man stayed on the ground until he didn't hear any more voices, and then walked until he found his companions. They knew then that the ircenrraats had seen him, so they wrapped him up and put him in his sled and pulled him so that he would not be seen again. Back in those days the ircenrraat could swim in the air, like it was water.

Sometimes if other people walked alone in the mountains, the ircenrraat would throw rocks at them, also. Wherever the rocks hit them, they would have ailments on their bodies in the future.

Ircenrraat are said to live inside the mountains or hills. Sometimes specific places are mentioned such as Pilcher Mountain and Nelson Island. Small toylike sleds or tools have been found in the hills on Nelson Island. Sometimes people might hear the ircenrraat and find a window to look inside their homes.

One time a man told about looking through the window and watching some ircenrraat dancing and singing. They looked just like little people. He thought he had been watching for only an hour or less, but when he looked down at himself and at his sled, and because his clothes had become old and his sled had become weathered he knew he had watched for more than a year.

Sometimes the ircenrraat might take a person down inside the mountain to their home. They would have the person spend the night, but when they went back out of the mountain, they would have been gone for a long time.

One time a man wearing a parka that was a patchwork of many different skins was taken down into the home of the ircenrraat. They wanted to know about each skin. Where had he caught this one? What about this one? And this one? The man said, each time, that was his father's catch, or that was his grandfather's, or his uncle's, or his cousin's, or his brother's catch, or another relative's. So the ircenrraat thought that he had many helpers. So they decided not to keep him but to let him go because he had many helpers who would be looking for him, and they were afraid of the helpers. So to let him go, he would have to go out one of three doors. The door in the middle would let him out. The lower one he would be too low and the top one he would be too high. Some of the ircenrraat urged him to go out the top or the bottom door, but one of the elders said not to mess with him but to let him go through the middle. So he went out the middle door and came back into our world and he had been gone more than a year.

Cingssiigat are mischievous little beings who, like enukins, come out at night, but they are tiny, and their heads are pointy. They wear little conical hats and use needles as canes. They talk but sound like little chirping birds. They are very strong and fast. They hide in cracks in the wall when people come close.

One time a man wanted to catch a cingssiigat. He hid in the room and was very still. He could hear them but not see them. But when he heard one very nearby, he grabbed and caught it. All the other little ones hid in the walls. Then he called to a boy to light the lamp. In the light, he could see the cingssiigat, and it looked like a tiny man. It had lost all its strength with the light, and the man began to tease it and hold it close to the flame. The boy was thinking very hard that the man should not do that! Because of what he did, afterwards, the man was not able to hunt, because all of his targets moved away from him. But because of what he thought, the boy grew up to be a great hunter, as all his targets seemed to be being herded toward him. Each was repaid by the cingssiliget according to his action or thought.

Although most of the stories about seeing and mingling with the small beings took place long ago, some are more recent.

One time on an August night in 1988, a group of teenagers was driving around the road outside of Nome and noticed a pulsating light in the rear-view mirror. Of course, they turned the car around to "check it out." When they got close to the light, they saw a humanlike figure that they described as "between two and four feet tall," with broad shoulders, very muscular, and surrounded by "an eerie, greenish luminescence." It took off down the road with the teenagers following, then it suddenly stopped, and the vehicle ran right over it and "flattened it out."

PHOTO © TOM WALKER, ACCENTALASKA.COM

Land otter and coyote, or are they ircenrraats?

They quickly drove back into town to find someone to verify their sighting. The new "witness" reported seeing the same little green man, now standing beside the road in the location where he had been run over! Another carload of teenagers also reported seeing a, or the, little green man and claimed that it had chased them. For a few days there was great speculation that the creatures were the mythical "little people" who had come out of the mountains and into town.

There are many, many myths that deal with interactions between little people and Native villagers. It is said that the stories began long, long ago when the earth was thin. They have been told and retold for generation after generation, and have helped to keep the long winter nights comfortable. The stories teach children not to go alone out on the tundra, where it might be dangerous. They teach children to be kind and generous to animals, on which the welfare of the village depends. They teach children to play and work together, which makes hard jobs easier. They teach children and remind elders of all the elements that make up their culture.

Are the stories real? Absolutely, they are real stories.

Are the stories true? Absolutely, they are true in the hearts of the people.

Did they actually happen? Well, the little green men story from Nome was a hoax. It didn't happen.

As for the others, they are open to interpretation by the reader.

CHAPTER 7

The Ice Worm Cometh

Robert Service's book of poetry, *Bar-Room Ballads*, first published in 1940, included a poem entitled "The Ice Worm Cocktail." By then Service was a household name, having published his first book of poetry in Canada in 1907. His *Song of the Sourdough* was a phenomenal bestseller, and with the money from it and his second book he was able to resign from his bank job to travel and write poetry full time.

Service once gave credit for his initial poem, "The Shooting of Dan McGrew," to the young editor of the *Whitehorse Star*, Elmer J. White. He was trying to decide on something to recite at a concert when White said, "Why don't you write a poem of your own for us?" Wherever Service got his inspiration for that first poem, he certainly based his poem, "The Ice Worm Cocktail" on a story from E. J. "Stroller" White.

E. J. White had come to the frozen north with the onslaught of gold rushers of 1898. He stopped in Skagway and worked for the *Skagway News* for a year or so, before moving on to Dawson in the Yukon Territory. In Dawson he worked for the *Klondike Nugget* and some other local papers, then moved on to Whitehorse for a few years. There he was editor and owner of the *Whitehorse Star*. In 1916 White returned to Alaska and a couple of years later settled in Juneau, where he published *Stroller's Weekly* until his death in 1930.

Stroller White was the first "columnist" in the far north. His column, *The Stroller,* first appeared in Dawson in 1900. From then on, he wrote about the little things and people whom he met along his way. He said he wrote about the "Sam brothers, Flot and Jet," and for the next thirty years he was the most quoted newspaperman, and his column the most copied, all over the North.

In many of his weekly columns from Juneau, he wrote about people and events from his Klondike days. In 1969 R. N. DeArmond, who had worked with White on *Stroller's Weekly,* compiled some of the "tales" from his columns into a book, *Stroller White, Tales of a Klondike Newsman.* One of those tales is "The Ice Worm Story."

It seems that during Stroller's early days as a reporter for the *Klondike Nugget,* there came, during a particularly bad winter, a horrendous blizzard that lasted for days and cut off the little town of Dawson from the outside world. There was little for the editor to write about in the paper except the depth of the snow. So he charged Stroller and the other cub reporter, Casey Moran, to "Go out and rustle up some news. Get me something that will make headlines and sell papers." So into the seventy-degree-below-zero snow-covered streets of Dawson went the two reporters.

Stroller, finding nothing of note from the numerous bar patrons whom he had interviewed, was headed back to the office when he heard the squeak of sled runners on the dry snow and had sudden inspiration.

Sitting down at his desk, Stroller typed out his fable of discovering a new species in a nearby glacier. He claimed that since the temperature had stayed at seventy below for more than two days, it had awakened the ice worms, which came out at the coldest temperatures and after a blue snow. Thousands and thousands of the worms had come out of the glaciers to bask in the "frigidity." There were so many that their chirping was keeping awake the residents of Dawson.

Although Stroller admitted that the story was a gag, the residents of Dawson kept pestering him for more information. He was forced to write another column, giving a description of the creatures and telling more about their habits. He explained that the worms came out from the glaciers and frolicked about in the cold at seventy-five to seventy degrees below zero. They grew rapidly and could grow to three and a half feet in twenty days. From sixty-eight to eighty-eight degrees below zero the worms are tasty, somewhat like Saddlerock oysters. But when the temperature rises to fifty below, they begin to fade away. Their incessant chirping comes from a whistle on the tail, and the head is always chomping away at the ice to make room for growth.

It seems that Stroller was destined to perpetuate his gag. By the next day the local bars were advertising "Ice Worm

Cocktails" for a dollar. The "worms" were encased in a block of ice behind the bar, and the bartender would chip one out and drop it in a drink. When Stroller was coerced into drinking one of the cocktails, the bartender whispered to him, "We couldn't get any of the real thing, so we faked 'em by poking spaghetti through gimlet holes in the ice and letting it swell. But for Pete's sake, don't tell any of the boys the difference."

Stroller's ice worms seemed to have a life of their own. His story was picked up and distributed to newspapers not only in Alaska and Canada, but even abroad. Everywhere, it seemed, his little gag was taken seriously, and he was inundated with requests for more information. The Society for Scientific Research, of London, England, asked that specimens be sent by mail immediately.

The May 30, 2008, edition of the *Whitehorse Star* included an article about the "Ice Worm Cocktail" from its archives. In 1907 the *Star* had published a letter sent to E. J. White, at the *Star,* from Cleveland Abbe, professor and editor, at the US Department of Agriculture. He asked:

I am interested in some of your letters, signed "The Stroller," as you seemed to have introduced a new term, "ice worms," which now belongs to English literature and must be mentioned in our dictionaries.

I should like to have a short paragraph stating the origin and history of this word and some account of the myths connected with it.

Of course, Stroller was delighted to answer Mr. Abbe. He included the aforementioned attributes of said ice worms and added a few pertinent facts, such as that the worms could be dried and kept to make soup when the winters were too mild for them to appear.

He concluded,

Incidentally, Mr. Abbe, you might mention in your dictionary that ice worms flourish best and that the tail whistle concert is loudest and most harmonious when the ice is covered with from three to five inches of blue snow.

The letter was signed:

Dictated by E. J. W.

Typewritten by Ann Jones

Mending of all kinds. Buttons sewed on while you wait.

And so, the Ice Worm entered into Alaska mythology. Barrett Willoughby, who wrote a book about notable Alaskans, included "Stroller" White, as "The Man Who Invented the Ice Worm."

"Stroller" White passed on in 1930, and he may or may not have heard by then that ice worms really do exist, although they are not exactly the way he had described them.

The existence of real ice worms was first noted back in 1887, even before Stroller described his "discovery." Glacial geologist George Frederick Wright came across the little critters while hiking on Muir Glacier, in Southeast Alaska. As daylight began to wane, the glacier suddenly came alive with thousands of tiny, black moving threads that, on closer inspection, proved to be worms. Dr. Wright wrote of them, "In shallower enclosures on the surface (of the glacier) containing water and a little dirt, worms about as large around as a small knitting needle are abundant."

Ten years later, on Mount Olympus in Washington state, photographer Asahel Curtis took pictures of worms that he referred to as "snow eels." Although there was some further research done before 1920, scientific curiosity about the critters lay mostly dormant until the 1970s.

Of course, those who spent time around the glaciers were aware of the worms, and the National Park Service had information about them. The Begich-Boggs Visitor Center at Portage Glacier just south of Anchorage opened in 1986 and displays live ice worms in a small desktop cooling tank at the center. Park Rangers lead two hikes each day to view the worms at the glacier.

These genuine ice worms belong to the same phylum and class as earthworms. Their scientific name is *Mesenchytraeus solifugus,* the latter meaning sun-avoiding. This is appropriate, as the worms appear at dusk and retreat back into the ice comes dawn. During their foraging time they feed on algae, possibly on pollen grains and other debris that are deposited on the glaciers by wind, and are also likely to eat live bacteria and fungi that inhabit the glaciers. The worms are three-quarters to one inch long and move along the ice by alternately contracting

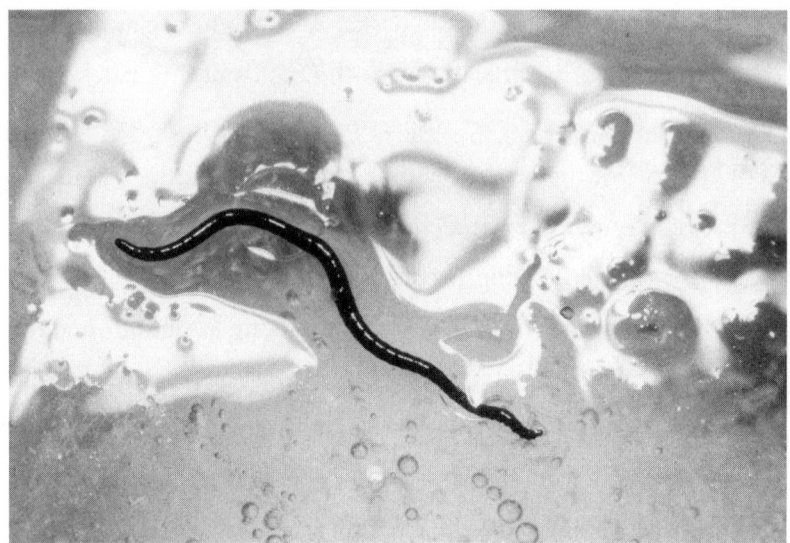

PHOTO © GLENN OLIVER, ACCENTALASKA.COM

Ice worms frolic on a glacier

longitudinal and circular muscles and with the help of "setae," little bristles that keep them from slipping backwards. It isn't clear exactly how the worms move through the hard glacier ice, but they appear to travel along tiny fissures between ice crystals. They easily burrow into the snow that covers glaciers but rely on the ice to keep them cold. The best temperature for ice worms is right about freezing, thirty-two degrees Fahrenheit. One fascinating aspect of these glacier organisms is that if the temperature of their surroundings goes below thirty-two degrees Fahrenheit, they actually become more energized, in contrast with other organisms that rapidly lose energy. But if the temperature rises to forty or forty-one degrees Fahrenheit, the worms begin to "melt" and eventually die. The worms could live for many days at forty degrees but not months. And if they are heated to room temperature for just a few hours, they will die.

One of the best authorities on the ice worm is Dr. Daniel Shain, a professor at Rutgers University. Dr. Shain first came upon them when he visited Alaska and noted a cartoon ice worm on a restaurant placemat. He, along with most tourists, assumed the worms were a joke, until he visited Portage Glacier, saw the exhibit at the Begich-Boggs Visitor Center, and was hooked. Since then he has studied them extensively, both in the laboratory and in the field.

Not only did Dr. Shain find the ice worms fascinating, but also NASA had such interest in potential comprehension of life on icy planets that they funded some of his research. Other scientists are investigating whether or not the ice worms' secrets might help develop a new way to store human organs for transplant, and they are being studied relevant to being indicators of climate change.

In 2008, Dr. Shain, along with Roman Dial, a professor from Alaska Pacific University, participated in a walking tour search for ice worms over some Alaska glaciers. A park ranger from Denali had told them of several places where he had seen worms some twenty years earlier. After trekking all through Denali searching the glaciers at dusk, they found no worms at all. They then proceeded to Learnard Glacier, near Whittier, where in the past Dr. Shain had seen lots of worms. This time they found some but not nearly as many as in other years.

"The worms were just about gone," Shain said. "We found about one worm every ten square meters; there used to be hundreds per square meter."

Learnard Glacier had shrunk a great deal since Dr. Shain had seen it a few years earlier. As glaciers shrink, they lose the snow that is imperative for the ice worms' survival, as it harbors the algae on which they feed. Some ice worms have been detected in snowfields that are actually disconnected from a glacier. Those worms have no way to traverse the area between the snow and their glacier, and they need the ice for their survival.

Ice worms that are classified as *Mesenchytraeus solifugus* have been found only in the glaciers of Southeast Alaska and glaciers in the Cascade Range in British Columbia, Washington, and Oregon. The species in Alaska has not been found in any other location. It is widely accepted that with the increase of global warming, polar bears may find themselves in danger as their ice melts, but the lowly glacier ice worm may also find it more difficult to survive in disappearing glaciers.

Nevertheless, as fascinating as is *Mesenchytraeus solifugus,* it will never catch the imagination of Alaskans as did Stroller White's Ice Worms, and the Ice Worm Cocktail.

In the 1930s, Juneau came alive dancing the "Ice Worm Wiggle Dance." The dance was accompanied by singing the "Ice Worm Wiggle" song, written by Carol Beery Davis. In 2002 the dance and song were resurrected as part of the Juneau-Douglas City Museum exhibit featuring entertainment in early Juneau.

In 1961 the small town of Cordova celebrated its first "Ice Worm Festival," to break the monotony of a long, dark, and frigid winter. The festival has continued to grow and is now celebrated on the first full weekend each February. Many exciting events and contests lead up to Friday, when Miss Ice Worm is crowned. On Saturday, besides the ever-popular "Survival Suit Race" across the chilly water in the harbor, there is the Ice Worm Parade. The parade is led, or sometimes ended, by a 150-foot-long ice worm with a dragon's head, propelled by numerous school children underneath the writhing body. There are usually about five hundred paraders, which leaves plenty of Cordovians to make an appreciative audience along the way.

And still to be found in Alaska are bartenders who will entice an unsuspecting cheechako to partake of one of Service's Ice Worm Cocktails.

CHAPTER 8

Permafrost—
Into the Ice Age, and Before

Anyone who has driven through Canada and on into Alaska along the Alcan Highway, or driven around the state on any of the three official State Highways, is familiar with the rolling, undulating pavement encountered along the way. The roadway dips and rises, slants to the left, then to the right. Traveling along it is like riding on a gigantic roller coaster. Then, some stretches are smooth and straight, lulling the driver into a false sense of security until the next unsuspected bounce occurs.

"Why don't these Alaskans take care of their roads!" the visitor asks himself. And the answer to that question is, Alaskans take amazingly good care of their roads, given what they have to work with! This old joke is understood in the far north: "There are two seasons, winter and road repair."

The real question is, what makes the roads so rough? And the answer to that is: permafrost.

Permafrost is defined as ground that has been frozen for at least two years. Some permafrost has been frozen for as long as ten thousand years, hiding inside it mysteries and treasures yet undiscovered. Some permafrost is just a few feet deep, but it has been found in places to be as deep as five thousand feet. Seasonal frost is ground that freezes in the winter and thaws in the summer. A layer of seasonal frost over permafrost is called the active layer. This layer would have different kinds of vegetation growing on it, depending on its depth.

If permafrost is found all over the ground surface of an area, it is called continuous. The areas in Alaska roughly from Bethel north to include both McGrath to the east and Nome to the west, then on past Kotzebue north to Barrow and east to the Canadian border are considered to be continuous. If permafrost exists only in some areas depending on vegetation, type of soil, moisture, and sun exposure, it is called discontinuous. A large area around Fairbanks and south to Anchorage and Valdez, including the Kenai Peninsula, is considered discontinuous. The rest of Alaska, including the Southeast, the Alaska Peninsula, and the Aleutians, is mostly free of any permafrost.

The frost heaves under the rolling roads are caused by segregated ice, that is, ice that forms within the active layer of seasonal frost. When the ice forms, it pushes up the soil under the pavement, and when it thaws, the soil moves down again. Since the freezing and thawing don't necessarily take place in the same location each time, the road responds as expected.

Another visible indication that permafrost is on the ground is found in the trees growing in a particular location. Black spruce is the only variety of tree that can grow over permafrost that is close to the surface. Trees growing directly over the frozen ground have less ability to absorb nutrients, as their roots have to grow along the ground rather than burrow down into the dirt. These trees are generally small and scraggly. Their wobbly, crooked appearance has led to the description "drunken forests." White spruce, aspen, and poplar trees are also seen nearby the black spruce, indicating that the permafrost is somewhat deeper in those areas.

The permafrost that exists around Fairbanks and other areas of interior Alaska was formed during the last Ice Age, which extended from roughly thirty-five thousand years ago up to about ten thousand years ago. During that time huge sheets of ice of varying depths extended across Canada and Greenland, parts of Alaska, and south to cover about one-fourth of the present United States. Most of the interior of Alaska was not covered by ice, but there were glaciers in the mountains of the Brooks Range and the Alaska Range. Silt from the glaciers washed down the rivers and raised the level of the permafrost. Everything in the ground was frozen, including all the plants and bones of animals. As the ground grew colder, well below freezing temperature in the winter, it cracked slightly. Water that came down from the glaciers filled the cracks and froze. Each spring the ice would melt slightly, and the process would repeat itself until there were large ice wedges inside the permafrost.

A slice through a typical permafrost area would show, from the top, an active layer of seasonal frost, then the permafrost made up of a layer of frozen silt containing ice, grasses, roots, and other plants, possibly some bones or other remnants of animals, a layer of frozen gravels, and, at the bottom, bedrock.

During the early 1960s, the US Army Engineer Research and Development Center's Cold Regions Research and Engineering Laboratory (CRREL) joined with the US Bureau of Mines to excavate a Permafrost Tunnel in Fox, Alaska, near Fairbanks.

Currently the tunnel is owned by CRREL, which operates it in cooperation with the University of Alaska Fairbanks Institute of Northern Engineering. The tunnel was excavated for the study of permafrost, geology, ice science, and the mining and construction techniques specific to permafrost environments. In 2011 excavation began on a new, larger tunnel to expand research opportunities such as building on permafrost and the issue of warming permafrost.

The original tunnel has two passages. The first one, called the adit, was dug horizontally through the layer of frozen silt. A vertical passage, called the winze, descended through the frozen gravels to the bedrock.

Construction of the tunnel was limited to the winter, and in the summer the tunnel was sealed to prevent the permafrost from thawing. A refrigeration unit was installed to maintain the summer temperature at twenty-four degrees. Of course, in the winter, no additional cooling is required. At the very beginning of the tunnel, excavation was through an active layer of seasonal frost, so structural support was provided by a semicircle of corrugated steel. Refrigeration coils placed in the soil there prevented the hillside from collapsing over the entrance. Once through the active layer and into the actual permafrost, the frozen silt and all it contained was strong enough to support the weight above, so nothing else was needed.

Walking into the tunnel is, literally, going back in time to the Ice Age. The theory of permafrost is there in actuality. There, in the silt layer, are plants, grasses, and roots, which were alive over ten thousand years ago. They froze so quickly, and remained frozen for so long, that a blade of grass plucked off the side of the tunnel still retains the green color from thousands of years ago.

Will tiny bits of frozen fauna help scientists learn about the existence of microbiotic life in the ice on faraway planets?

Also in the soil frozen in the tunnel, too tiny to be seen, are ice lenses that make up over half of the volume of the walls. Most noticeable in the walls are the large ice wedges. The largest one in the tunnel is eighteen feet wide and thirty-five feet tall. This frozen silt layer is about sixty feet thick.

Descending through the tunnel's gravel layer, the walls divulge more secrets. Hidden among the aggregate are bones, some of dinosaurs from as long ago as the Cretaceous period, and some from Ice Age animals, such as steppe bison or wooly mammoths. Certainly the dinosaur bones were washed down from soil layers where they had lain for millions of years. The more recent bones, only thousands of years old, were probably also washed into the gravels by rivers bringing them from places far away, as they appeared to be randomly distributed and not together from one skeleton.

The permafrost layer around Fairbanks has yielded other exciting discoveries, also. In 1979, Walter and Ruth Roman and their sons were using a hydraulic mining hose to wash away silt that covered the gravel on their placer gold mining claim. They uncovered what turned out to be the carcass of an Ice Age steppe bison buried in the frozen muck. Fortunately, they realized they had found something special and contacted the University of Alaska, Fairbanks.

Paleontologist Dale Guthrie was able to rescue the frozen carcass by a complicated series of carefully hewing out the head, then the rest of the carcass, and refreezing the parts in the school's laboratory. The whole carcass was covered with a chalky substance when it was discovered. The mineral, vivianite, had been produced when the phosphorus in the bison's tissue reacted with iron in the soil. When it was exposed to the air, it turned blue, so the bison was named Blue Babe, after Paul Bunyan's big blue ox.

Study of the carcass revealed that the bison died about thirty-six thousand years ago after being attacked by an Ice Age lion. It died in the winter; the carcass froze, and then was eventually encased in frozen soil that became permafrost.

The bison's bones were frozen but not fossilized! In the

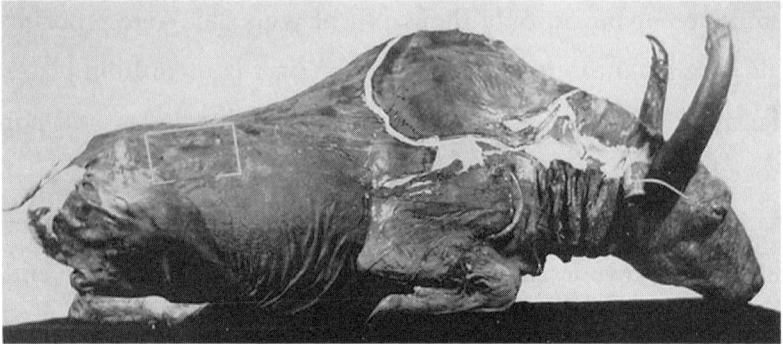

COURTESY OF WWW.BENBOYD.COM

Blue Babe, the steppe bison extracted from the permafrost near Fairbanks

modern world of DNA, will scientists be able to utilize material from an extinct species to recreate it?

In an amazing bit of taxidermy, Blue Babe was reconstructed using its own skin, and can be seen in a glass case at the University of Alaska Museum in Fairbanks. The bison is resting on its folded legs, just as it was found.

In the early 1960s while the Permafrost Tunnel was being constructed, the new Alaska Goldrush was beginning across the northern part of the state—the search for oil.

A young geologist working for Shell Oil, Robert Liscomb was doing fieldwork along the Colville River in 1961, mapping and collecting samples. He collected both rock and fossil samples, marked them carefully as to their location, noted them in his journal, and then sent them on to the Shell Oil laboratory for analysis. Unfortunately, Liscomb was killed in a rockslide the following year, and his samples and notes sat on shelves in the Shell Archives. It was not until 1983 that Liscomb's work was rediscovered and the fossils identified as hadrosaur bones. Hadrosaurs were large, bi-pedal (walked on two hind legs) herbivorous, "duck-billed" dinosaurs from the late Cretaceous period. The area where he found them was located in bluffs along the Coleville River, and the bone bed discovered there was consequently named the Liscomb Bone Bed in his honor.

Liscomb's hadrosaur fossils were the first discovery of dinosaurs in the arctic. It was well documented that there were fossils. There had been whole skeletons of wooly mammoths unearthed, as well as numerous fossils attributed to other Pleistocene, or Ice Age, animals. But it had long been believed, in the paleontology world, that dinosaurs were unable to adapt and exist in the frigid polar regions. Here, though, lay the proof that they were there.

The area of northern Alaska, known as the North Slope, is entirely covered under the surface by permafrost that is hundreds of feet deep. The Liscomb Bone Bed is at the base of one-hundred-foot-high bluffs along the Colville River south of Umiat and completely embedded in permafrost. It is three feet thick and about six-hundred feet long. At this time, no one knows exactly how far back into the bluffs it goes. Of course, the bones that are exposed at the edge of the bed are more easily extracted, as the permafrost there is thawing as it meets the warm air.

Roland Gangloff, curator of earth sciences for the University of Alaska in Fairbanks, began fieldwork in the Liscomb bed in 1987 and after the first few years oversaw the project until his retirement in 2003. Gangloff brought field teams of students from the university, as well as volunteers from many other places. He set up an excellent summer program for teachers interested in furthering their knowledge of paleontology. Because the weather in the allotted time for summer studies, roughly mid-July to late August, was often severe, some years there were only twelve to fifteen days of actual field work.

As more and more hadrosaur bones were taken out of the permafrost and transported back to the museum in Fairbanks, it became clear to Gangloff that "this is going to be one of the densest bone yards ever."

Gangloff noted that the bone bed consisted of primarily young hadrosaurs, based on the development of the bone structures. He postulated that the bones had come from one "event," which he described relating it to similar events in the present. The theory is that many animals, a herd, were crossing a river that was at flood stage, possibly a flash flood, and the adult animals were able to get across but the juveniles drowned. Then, all of the bodies were washed downstream and came together in one area. Over time, bones of other dinosaurs were washed down into the same general location, where they lay for millions of years, eventually being covered by thick layers of sediment, fossilized, and frozen into permafrost.

In his book, *Dinosaurs under the Aurora,* Gangloff goes on to posit how the hadrosaurs and other dinosaurs came to be this far north in Alaska. Plant fossils and other evidence indicate that the climate in the Cretaceous period was far milder than it is today, so it would not be hard to imagine that dinosaurs could have existed there. One theory is that they migrated south. Fossils of many known dinosaurs are found in Alaska, but there have not been any of lizards or reptiles such as those found in Montana and Alberta. So another theory is that the dinosaurs were warm-blooded, not cold-blooded as has been assumed. But the evidence hidden in the permafrost is clear; dinosaurs lived in Alaska!

Gangloff describes the difficulty and danger of working in the permafrost. First, the permafrost had to be penetrated far enough into the bluff to set up a quadrat, or working area a yard square and level; then that quadrat would be excavated, bit by bit, using trench shovels, rock hammers, chisels, knives, ice picks, and brushes. The top of the bed held small bones, teeth, and bone fragments. All of these had to be mapped and recorded before the larger (and more interesting) bones could be examined. Teams of two or three individuals worked each quadrat. There was constant danger from landslides as the exposed permafrost thawed and dropped down the bluffs.

In 1989 the temperatures were warmer than usual and there were more landslides. Two visiting scientists from Australia, Thomas Rich and Patricia Vickers-Rich, thought there had to be a safer way to work the bone bed. Over the next several years Thomas Rich collaborated with Gangloff to find it. The idea was to build a tunnel through the permafrost, somewhat like the one the CRREL operated in Fox but much smaller. Over the next twenty years or so, they worked off and on to get funding to fulfill that dream. It wasn't until 2007, however, that the tunnel was finally brought into being. By then Gangloff had retired from his position and was no longer involved with the summer field work there. The primary funding for the tunnel turned out to have come from a media group put together to film a documentary with Thomas Rich about dinosaur bone discovery. As it turned out, a ten-foot by ten-foot tunnel was drilled about thirty feet into the bone bed. The bones that were recovered were, on the whole, in better condition than the ones from nearer the edge of the bed, which had been subjected over the millions of years to thawing and refreezing. However, the expense and difficulty involved in building and maintaining the tunnel made it impractical to consider it as a research tool in the future.

Permafrost continues to be an Alaska mystery. Scientists wonder if they can solve age-old mysteries from what has already been discovered, and they wonder what more can be found in its depths. Engineers wonder how to make building on it safer. And the rest of Alaskans wonder if the roads will ever be smooth.

CHAPTER 9

The Earth Rumbles and Blows Smoke

It was a perfectly clear and sunny morning in Sitka on April 1, 1974. As the citizens awoke and began to go about their routines, they noticed something menacing in the distance. Some thirteen miles to the west on the southern end of Kruzof Island, the extinct volcano, Mount Edgecumbe, was emitting a thick plume of smoke! Was it about to erupt? Surely not! The volcano had been dormant for more than four thousand years—give or take a few hundred.

Telephones "rang off their hooks" at the local police and fire stations. The Coast Guard station in Sitka alerted the admiral in the Juneau office who sent a helicopter pilot to investigate. As the pilot approached the crater and was able to see directly down into it, he began to laugh! Stacked up just below the edge was a pile of old rubber tires, burning and producing the heavy black smoke. Spray-painted in the snow were fifty foot high letters spelling out April Fool.

Sitka resident Porky Bickar had first thought up the prank in 1971. He assembled all of the necessary equipment but then

W. A. Hesse taking moving pictures of Katmai Volcano

Library of Congress Prints and Photographs Division Washington, DC 20540 USA
Copyright 1913 by M. Horner. Gift; Mrs. W. Chapin Huntington; 1951.

had to wait another three years for the weather to cooperate enough to accomplish the event. Pulling off the prank required two huge slings that would hold at least fifty old tires each and some oily rags, sterno, and diesel oil, not to mention a helicopter pilot who would agree to transport it all. Porky and the pilot had to make two trips over to the volcano, assisted on the ground by two other cohorts. The preparation went off without a hitch, and the result was exactly what Porky had in mind. His great prank was appreciated and enjoyed by all, including the officials, and is still listed as one of the ten best April Fool's hoaxes of all times.

But volcanoes are no laughing matter to Alaskans. Sitting on the edge of the great "Ring of Fire" that encircles the Pacific Ocean, Alaska has experienced the devastation that can result from volcanic eruptions for as long as the land has existed.

A very old myth from the extinct Tsetsaut tribe tells about "a long time ago" when fire came through the air like a huge animal. It had fire on its face and on its back and from its paws.

According to an Aleut legend, Chuginadak, the Goddess of Fire, lives inside the volcanoes along the islands that make up the Aleutians. When the ground shakes and rolls, it is because she is restless and uncomfortable lying in one position all the time. When she is angry, she throws fire and smoke from the tops of the mountains.

An old Tlingit myth tells that man received fire when Raven stole a firebrand (burning stick) from the top of a mountain where the Fire God was throwing fire. A more recent version of that story identifies the fire where Raven got the firebrand as coming from a fumarole in the "Valley of Ten Thousand Smokes."

There are forty volcanoes located in the Aleutian Volcanic Arc, which stretches from Spurr at the top of Cook Inlet all along the Aleutian Islands to Kiska, on Kiska Island, which is close to Attu, the last island in the chain. All of these volcanoes except Dutton, at the southwest end of the Alaska Peninsula, and Iliamna, near Cook Inlet, have erupted at least once in the last two hundred years!

Volcano eruptions are measured with the volcanic explosivity index, or VEI. The scale is 1 to 7, with 7 being the kind that happen "every eon or so." The only VEI 7 actually recorded was the Indonesian eruption of Mount Tambora in 1815.

The 1912 eruption of Novarupta, across Shelikof Strait from Kodiak Island, was the largest volcanic eruption in the twentieth century. One of the five largest in recorded history, it was given a VEI measurement of 6. Amazingly, there was no loss of life, as inhabitants of the few villages near the mountain had fled to the coasts when the earthshaking rumblings increased.

Harry Kaiakokonok was a six-year-old boy watching the mountain from a fish camp on Kaflia Bay, thirty-two miles east of Novarupta. Many years later he described the mysterious event.

"BLA-LOOM! It is the mountain. The mountain is doing something. . . . Dark didn't come all of a sudden, it comes gradually. Getting darker and darker, and pretty soon, pitch black. So black even if you put your hand two or three inches from your face outside you can't see it 'cause it was so dark. And then the people started to gather up."

Although none of the villagers had experienced an eruption in their lifetimes, oral tradition had prepared them. One old man in Katmai told his neighbors, "Put away as much water as you can and store it, reserve it. Wherever ashes come down there will be no water to drink anywhere. Turn your boats upside down. They will be filled with ash."

The eruption continued for at least three days and shot about three cubic miles of magma into the air. An ash cloud rose one-hundred thousand feet, or almost twenty miles, into the air. Ash fell as far away as Seattle, and the cloud drifted as far away as Africa and caused a cooler than normal summer that year in the temperate zones of the northern hemisphere. Ash up to seven hundred feet thick in places covered an area of forty square miles of the valley. Jets of steam and gas spewed from vents in the earth, earning the name "Valley of Ten Thousand Smokes." Over the years the smoking vents diminished, leaving no fumarole activity visible today.

Father Bernard Hubbard first explored this mysterious Valley of Smokes in 1929. Father Hubbard was the head of the geology department at the University of Santa Clara in California. Every year after the end of the term, he shed his priestly garments in favor of boots and backpacks and headed out for Alaska. Accompanied by a small band of students and carrying equipment for both still and moving photography, Father Hubbard traipsed across glacier fields, up and down mountain ranges, and through the tundra. His explorations had led him to be dubbed the "Glacier Priest." At the end of each summer he traveled all across the Lower 48, showing his films and lecturing about the unbelievable wonders he had seen in the wild.

Father Hubbard described the volcanoes on the Alaska Peninsula as "a geological paradise." His little troop of four explorers traveled across the smoking valley, camping in fissures and cooking over fumaroles. He told Barrett Willoughby, who wrote about him in her book, *Alaskans All,* "When I saw the Valley of the Smokes and Katmai's crater last year, I was convinced Alaska had nothing further in the way of surprises to offer. But on my return from that trip, I learned of the Moon Craters!"

Father Hubbard was referring to the two mountains, Aniakchak and Veniaminoff, which lay along the Alaska Peninsula one hundred fifty miles to the west of the Katmai. The crater, or caldera, itself is thirty square miles in area. Veniaminoff, some eighty miles away, has a crater of twenty-five square miles.

For many years Father Hubbard had harbored the hope of finding on the earth's crust the same kind of crater formation that can be observed looking at the moon. So the following summer he and four other stalwart explorers set off for the moon craters. These two mountains had been explored a few years earlier and had been declared dead volcanoes.

The group spent several weeks trekking up to and inside, first Aniakchak. They found an almost mythological land of flowers, birds, mammals, a beautiful lake full of fish, and fabulously colored geologic formations. They found a dormant volcano in the center of the crater and, to their surprise, a miniature "valley of smokes." Next, they trudged valiantly off toward Veniaminoff. After struggling through severe Alaska storms coming wildly off the Bering Sea, they made their way to the top of the mountain where they could look down inside the crater. There they were rewarded with the view of a crater filled with an icy glacier. A white mountain rose from the middle of the ice, and, as they watched, the cone spewed out a bit of coal-black ash. The two "dead moon craters" were, mysteriously, alive.

During the rest of that year and into 1931, several volcanoes in the Aleutian Volcanic Arc made themselves known by erupting with emissions ranging from black plumes of smoke and shafts of fire to flowing lava. Father Hubbard was hoping for a major eruption to explore, and it came from Aniakchak just as he and a crew of three students were preparing to revisit that crater. The eruption began on May 1 with plumes of white smoke then explosions of lava bombs and ash clouds towering at least twenty thousand feet into the sky and traveling more than 350 miles. The eruptions continued for ten days, when a final explosion shook the surrounding country and sent ashes into the air in such volume that it created hours of darkness for a distance of sixty miles from the volcano. After a few days respite another eruption began on May 20. This one lasted only a few days before lava domes began to form in the new vents and eruption ceased.

Father Hubbard and his crew spent the rest of the summer exploring the devastation that was now Aniakchak crater.

The idyllic land from the previous summer was no more. Father Hubbard equated it as having seen "Paradise Lost after the Paradise Found" the previous year. He wrote about looking over the edge of the crater for the first time.

"Silence. Nobody wanted to speak. There was the new Aniakchak, but it was the abomination of desolation, it was the prelude of hell. Black walls, black floor, black water, deep black holes and black vents; it fairly agonized the eye to look at it."

His lectures for the following year (and after) showed heartbreaking comparison photos of wildflowers versus black ash fields and snow-covered glaciers, now black ice.

Although Father Hubbard regarded his exploits as scientific explorations, his data and measurements were not all that accurate or complete by today's standards. However, his lectures and breathtaking photographs brought new awareness of the mysteries that were to be found in the soon-to-be state of Alaska.

Amazingly, in all Alaska eruptions known in written history, there has been only one death directly attributed to a volcanic eruption. That occurred in 1944, when there was a small troop of soldiers stationed on uninhabited Chuginadak Island, where Mount Cleveland is located. On June 10, one of the soldiers went for a walk. But perhaps Chuginadak Goddess of Fire was not happy to have the soldiers there. For suddenly the mountain began to smoke, and the soldiers felt the ground shake, so they went after their comrade along the beach. They followed until his footsteps disappeared where a mudslide had come off the mountain, and he was never seen again. The soldiers sheltered themselves while the eruption continued for three days, and they were then transferred permanently from the island. Although there are no inhabitants on this lonely island, a figure dressed in military garb might be seen through the mist, strolling along the rocky shores.

Mount Cleveland has erupted some twenty-six or twenty-seven times since 1893. Significantly, this century it has increased activity, erupting twelve times in as many years. In 2001 it produced a seven-mile-high ash plume that disrupted air traffic in the area.

Augustine, Iliamna, Redoubt, and Spurr are the four volcanoes in or near Cook Inlet. These cones are monitored closely and cause much concern because they are near large population centers, such as Anchorage and the Kenai Peninsula. Also, much of the air traffic coming in and out of Ted Stevens airport in Anchorage normally passes right over them. All of them except Iliamna have been very active in the last few decades.

Ash clouds traveling over populated areas are more than an inconvenience; they are extremely dangerous. Volcanic ash is made up of infinitesimal bits of pulverized rocks, minerals, and volcanic glass. It is, first and foremost, unhealthy to inhale. It is also disruptive to engines of all kinds, especially airplanes and other vehicles. It can be pulled into vents for oil stoves and other machinery, causing complete shutdown.

Of course, there are many different types of natural disasters in the world, such as floods, tornadoes, and hurricanes. One thing that they have in common is that they can be predicted with relative accuracy. People come to expect "hurricane season," or the time of year for monsoons for example. Knowing the events are probable doesn't mean that they are preventable, but at least there is warning so that people have some chance to escape them. The mystery of Alaska's volcanoes is not knowing when they might erupt—or after they have started spewing ash, when they will stop! Some lie dormant for hundreds of years, while others come to life intermittently.

In January of 1976 Augustine erupted for three days, sending into the sky an ash cloud that was seen as far away as Arizona. Ash fell on the Kenai Peninsula, and hot gas clouds swept down the slopes of the mountain, destroying a small research hut that was fortunately unmanned during the winter. The blast carried temperatures higher than five hundred degrees that seared wood outside the hut and melted plastic objects inside.

Ten years later Augustine came to life again, covering Cook Inlet and the Kenai Peninsula with layers of ash for two days and leaving dust in the air over Cook Inlet for two days more before the wind changed and blew it away.

In January of 2006 a VEI 3 eruption of Augustine again triggered ash plumes that drifted over Anchorage and the Kenai Peninsula. For several days the ash settled on the ground and occasional ash plumes shot into the air, causing many airline reschedulings and delays. At one point there was concern that a major eruption was imminent, but the violent activity slowed, with only some low-level eruptions continuing through April.

Iliamna is supposed to be dormant currently but exhibited what might have been small eruptions in 1947, 1952, and 1953. Otherwise, its activity has been merely non-eruptive activities such as small white plumes of steam and gas emitted from fumaroles near its peak and flurries of small earthquakes.

On December 14, 1989, after having been inactive for about twenty-five years, Redoubt sprang alive with a number of explosions sending ash over the whole Cook Inlet region and Southcentral Alaska. It disrupted much of the holiday air traffic. As airlines rushed to get their planes in the air and out of the Alaska skies, some lucky passengers were able to leap into action and make the flight when notified that their scheduled departure time had been moved up several hours.

The following day, December 15, a KLM Boeing 747 was headed into the Anchorage airport when it flew directly into a volcanic ash plume. The mysterious plume was difficult to see and identify until the plane was actually inside it and began to fill up with smoke. As the pilot realized what had happened, he tried to ascend out of the cloud, but suddenly all four engines stopped, and the plane began to fall nose down. As the volcanic glass of the ash plume was sucked into the engines, it began to melt, coating the inside of the engine and giving the impression that it was overheating, so the automatic shutdown began. The 747 plunged from twenty-five thousand feet down to twelve thousand feet in eight minutes, before the pilot was able to restart all four engines and land his craft safely!

The 1989 Redoubt eruption continued into 1990 off and on for about six months, spreading ash over the Kenai Peninsula, disrupting air traffic, and causing many days of lost labor and school closures.

Then again in March of 2009 Redoubt began erupting. The seismic activity lasted until late May. Advisories were posted, and communities as far away as Valdez and Mat-Su Valley, as well as Anchorage and the Kenai Peninsula, were coated with ash and tephra. At least fifteen days in March and April saw some sort of seismic event, with one ash cloud reaching sixty-five thousand feet into the sky. The activity continued until late May, when it decreased. The rest of 2009 was relatively quiet on Redoubt until the end of the year when a few small earthquake swarms occurred.

Spurr is the highest volcano in the Aleutian Volcanic Arc, and the closest one to Anchorage. In known history, Spurr has erupted only twice, in 1953 and again in 1992. In both of those eruptions, ash fell on Anchorage and surrounding areas

Sometimes eruptions of volcanoes give some warning before an actual event. There are days, sometimes weeks or months, of small tremblers and/or small steam emissions. Alaskans who live in the predicted path of any ash cloud know to prepare for several days or more of inconvenience and unexpected difficulties. Those who can, leave for the duration. Those who can't, buckle down with extra water, shovels, and good books. True Alaskans consider dealing with volcanoes just part of the mystery of living in "The Great Land."

After the 1989–1990 eruption of Redoubt, the Alaska Volcano Observatory (AVO) devised a Level of Concern Color Codes for volcanoes in Alaska:

Green: Volcano is in its normal "dormant" state.

Yellow: Volcano is restless. Seismic activity is elevated. Potential for eruptive activity is increased.

Orange: Small ash eruption expected or confirmed. Plume(s) not likely to rise above twenty-five thousand feet above sea level.

Red: Large ash eruptions expected or confirmed. Plume likely to rise about twenty-five thousand feet above sea level.

The AVO sends timely warnings of volcanic unrest and potential eruptions to the Federal Aviation Administration, the National Weather Service, the Alaska Division of Emergency Services, local military bases, state offices, radio and TV stations, news wire services, and others. The information is also posted on the AVO website.

As of this writing, August 2012, Cleveland Volcano is "Level of Concern Color Code Orange." Iliamna has, since March 2012, been "Level of Concern Color Code Yellow." All of the other volcanoes in the Aleutian Volcanic Arc are "Level of Concern Color Code Green."

Hopefully Chuginadak is comfortable in her current position, and nothing will make her angry in the foreseeable future!

CHAPTER 10

Denali: Who Climbed It? Who Didn't?

Alaska Athabascan tribes had several names for the mountain towering above the Alaska Range, all of which meant "The Great One." Deenaalee was the one most commonly used, eventually becoming Denali.

To the Ten'a people in the Tanana Valley, the mountain is the throne of the Shaman Sa, Master of Life, who sends the warm season to defeat the demon snow,

To bring sweet rains, budding trees,

Spawning fish, and golden bees

In 1897 prospector William Dickey, writing about his Alaska adventures to the *New York Sun,* proposed that the giant mountain, which he estimated correctly to be over twenty thousand feet high, be named after William McKinley, the Republican presidential nominee. He rendered a map of the area, with the mountain noted as "Mt. McKinley, twenty thousand feet," and that name became official. Still, many Alaskans refer to it by the Native name.

The discovery of this highest mountain in North America caused quite a stir in the exploration community. Although it was not as high as Tibetan peaks, it rose higher from its base than did those that began from lofty plateaus. It was extremely remote, and any expedition would travel under extreme conditions. Certainly the explorer who was the first to conquer this mythical behemoth of a mountain would gain fame and fortune.

In 1903 Judge James Wickersham led four other valiant climbers on the first attempt to scale the mountain, approaching it from the north. They traveled from May to July, but got no higher than eight thousand feet when forced to turn back because of soft snow and avalanche danger.

Another attempt was also made in 1903, this an expedition led by Dr. Frederick A. Cook. Dr. Cook had made two successful sojourns into Greenland, one with then Lieutenant Robert A. Peary, and had lectured extensively about Eskimos and their culture. He had also traveled to Antarctica as an expedition physician. He considered himself to be quite the explorer, and his secret goal was to mount his own expedition to reach the North Pole before Peary did. In order to be taken seriously enough to do that, he knew he had to do something spectacular on his own to attract sponsors for such an undertaking. He decided that being the first to climb Mount McKinley would be just the ticket.

The expedition was doomed from the beginning, as the group of six travelers didn't start north from Cook Inlet until late June. Traveling northwest and around the Alaska Range, It was August 29 by the time they arrived at the point chosen to begin the actual climb up the north side of the mountain. The second day they camped at 10,800 feet elevation, but were stymied by a gigantic ridge of steep granite ledges. One member was quoted, "It ain't that we can't find a way, takin' chances. There ain't no way at all!" Although Cook failed in his attempt to climb McKinley, he did succeed in traveling all the way around it, as they made their way to the southeast, back around, and down the Chulitna River past what are now called Eldridge and Ruth Glaciers, and back to Cook Inlet. This feat would not be duplicated for fifty years.

Determined now, Dr. Cook put together another climbing expedition in 1906. Herschel Parker and Belmore Browne were two of the seven-member group that started out from Tyonek, on Cook Inlet, at the end of May. Ed Barrill, a Montana horse-packer with no mountaineering experience at all, was along to care for the stock. After struggling for several weeks to find a passageway up the mountain from the southeast, the expedition split into two groups. Barrill and another man stayed with the horses at Susitna Station while the others went on downriver to Tyonek, where Cook was to meet a friend coming to hunt game. Parker traveled back to New York. When Cook's friend wired that he was not coming, Cook returned to where Barrill was waiting. He had decided to make one more try to conquer the mountain from that southeast side, but declined Browne's offer to accompany him.

Imagine the surprise when, on September 22, Dr. Cook arrived back at Susitna Station announcing that he and Barrill had made it to the top of McKinley! He claimed that they had done the actual climb in twelve days, taking eight days to ascend and only four to return to their base camp near Ruth Glacier.

When Belmore Browne heard the rumor of this claim, he commented that it was as absurd as "a man to report that he had walked the distance from Brooklyn Bridge to Grant's tomb (10.8 miles) in ten minutes."

Cook produced photographs purporting to have been taken at and from the top of the peak. One showed a triumphant Barrill standing atop a precipice holding an American flag against a light sky. Cook's journal of the climb after passing Ruth Glacier was scant on topographic features and heavy on inspirational description. He claimed that from the top of the mountain could be seen the Arctic Circle, the Pacific Ocean, "narrow silvery bands" that were the Tanana and Yukon rivers, as well as the volcanoes, Redoubt, Illiamna, and Chinabora, and the Kenai Peninsula all to the south. Subsequent successful climbers debunked the possibility of viewing the sights "seen" by Cook.

Nevertheless, the general public was eager to endorse a new accomplishment by an already established adventurer and explorer. So Dr. Frederick A. Cook returned to civilization as the conquering hero of the tallest mountain in North America. He lectured successfully around the country about his accomplishment.

A *Harper's Monthly Magazine* article containing many of his photographs further cemented his believability with the populace.

Even though there was still some argument about the truth of Cook's claims, the controversy seemed to die down, only to reappear with a vengeance a couple of years later.

Cook had managed to assemble an expedition team in 1907 to launch an assault on the North Pole. On September 1, 1909, he was sailing from Greenland and able to send a telegram stating that on April 28, 1908, he had, indeed, reached the North Pole. This was greeted with great excitement and exhilaration, and Cook was again being hailed as a conquering hero. This adulation lasted less than a week. On September 6, a telegram was received from Robert Peary, sent from Labrador, that he, himself, had reached the North Pole on April 6, 1909, and that Cook was a liar. Peary went on to say, "Cook's story should not be taken too seriously. The two Eskimos who accompanied him say he went no distance north and not out of sight of land."

Now all of the doubters of Cook's McKinley conquest story came out of the woodwork. Ed Barrill even signed an affidavit stating that Dr. Cook had not reached the top of the mountain and had written false captions for the photographs. The debate raged near and far across the country. The photograph that he purported to have taken atop the mountain was proven to be fake. Apparently Cook's claim to have climbed the mythical Denali became a myth itself, waiting to be debunked.

One evening in the fall of 1909, the subject was being discussed in Bill McPhee's Washington Saloon in Fairbanks, Alaska. Tom Lloyd had mined in Kantishna near the foothills of McKinley for several years and opined that not only could the mountain be climbed, but also that he and some other miners he knew could do it. McPhee put up $500, and two others, Gust Peterson and E. W. Griffin, stepped forward with another $500 each, and the game was on. Griffin even supplied a flag to be hoisted at the summit.

The next few months were spent putting together the team that would make the climb, planning the route, and gathering supplies. Tom Lloyd chose three sourdoughs who worked with him mining in Kantishna, Peter Anderson, Charles McGonagall, and Billy Taylor. Thus was formed the "Lloyd Party," off to debunk Cook's myth.

These men who planned to climb The Great One were neither mountaineers nor climbers. They were simply Alaskans who believed that if the mountain were destined to be climbed, it should be climbed first by Alaskans, not by some cheechakos with their silk underwear and fancy gear. Over their long winter underwear they wore bib overalls, shirts, mittens, and light duck parkas, not fur-lined. On their feet were shoepacs (rubber boots with laced leather uppers) for trekking and Native moccasins with metal "creepers" tied on them for climbing the ice. Mountaineering equipment consisted of snowshoes, handmade crampons, and long pike poles with steel hooks, no ropes, or other climbing gear. Their supplies included bacon, beans, flour, sugar, dried fruits, and butter, as well as the pans, stove, and tents to make up a "general outfit" for traveling in the wilderness. In the lower elevations they also had caribou meat for steaks and making stews. They initially traveled with a dog team, three or four horses, and a mule.

In addition to supplies and gear, the expedition also carried a fourteen-foot-long spruce pole, from which they planned to fly a six-foot by twelve-foot American flag at the top of the mountain to signify their success.

The expedition set out from Fairbanks before the end of the year, to reconnoiter and set the route for their climb. The men traveled southeast about sixty miles to the Nenana River, then on to their mines in Kantishna where they began assembling their supplies. Both Tom Lloyd and Pete Anderson had spent enough time traveling the valleys and hills that they could lead the group across the foothills to their first camp, the Willows, which they set up in February at the mouth of Cache Creek.

Charlie McGonagall had observed the Muldrow Glacier from his cabin and explored it extensively while mining up on Moose Creek, and he was sure that traveling up between its steep walls was the way to access the summit. He and Anderson scouted from the Cache Creek Camp and found a pass that took them to

on the slope of
Mt. McKinley

P277-004-089, Courtesy of Alaska State Library, Wickersham State Historic Sites Photograph Collection

Charlie McGonagall and Tom Lloyd of the All Alaskan Sourdough Expedition . . .
at their 15,000-foot-level camp on Mount McKinley

the glacier. The first week in March was spent ferrying supplies to the next camp at the edge of the glacier. From there they set stakes across the glacier to mark the way to the final camp.

On March 29, 1910, the whole party traversed the glacier, with the dog team carrying supplies, and made camp at its head. This was the Tunnel Camp, at eleven thousand feet, from which the ascent on the summit would begin. For the next two days, Anderson, Taylor, and McGonagall made final preparation for the climb. Tom Lloyd cooked doughnuts that the three would carry with them to the top.

At the time of this part of the climb, Billy Taylor was twenty-two years old. He had his birthday in March while on the glacier. Charlie McGonagall was forty-three and Pete Anderson was forty. Lloyd was the oldest of the group, at fifty, and heavy-set. It is likely that he also suffered from altitude sickness. He did not attempt to make the last dash to the top and was waiting back down the mountain at the Willows camp.

On April 1 the three sourdoughs set out for the summit but were turned back by raging weather.

On April 3 they started out again, leaving camp a little after 3:00 a.m. They wore their moccasins with the handmade crampons (creepers) and carried pole-axes, double-bitted axes, and climbing poles. In knapsacks they packed some rope to tie down the flagpole, the flag, candles, a camera, doughnuts, and each a thermos of hot chocolate. And, of course, they carried the fourteen-foot spruce pole.

At first they cut steps with the axes but then disdained that method for just the use of their climbing poles and creepers. They climbed steadily. At about five hundred feet from the summit, McGonagall handed off the pole to one of the others, sat down and rested, then returned to camp.

At approximately 3:00 p.m. Pete Anderson and Billy Taylor stepped onto the top of the North Peak of Mount McKinley. In an interview with Norman Bright some twenty-seven years later, Taylor described the top as "little pinnacles of rock from four to six inches high. But generally speaking it was just a mass of ice."

Because the top was ice, they had to raise the pole about twelve feet below the actual summit, where there was a pile of rocks. Taylor described the "cairn."

"We dug down in the ice with a little axe we had and built a pyramid of fifteen inches high, and we dug down in the ice, so the pole had a support of about thirty inches, and it was held by four guy lines—just cotton ropes. We fastened the guy lines to little spurs of rocks."

The climbers didn't realize that the South Peak was actually a bit higher than the one they had climbed until they stood on the top. They had chosen to ascend the North Peak because they thought that it could more easily be seen from Fairbanks. The flag, too, was planted on the north of the peak for the same reason. In reality, there was no way that the flag could have been seen from Fairbanks, even with a powerful telescope, because of

atmospheric interference. Nevertheless, they considered themselves to have reached the top of the mountain.

The three climbers descended to the Tunnel Camp, arriving there about dusk. The incredible dash to the top and back
had taken only eighteen hours. After resting a bit, they made
their way back down past the first glacier camp to where Tom
Lloyd was awaiting their arrival at the Willows.

After their successful climb, the three miners went back to
work at their various holdings in Kantishna. It was good working
weather, and they had much to do, and not seekers of publicity,
they were quite willing to let Tom Lloyd take the news back to
Fairbanks. It was, after all, Lloyd's party.

Tom Lloyd then traveled into Fairbanks, arriving there on
April 11, to tell his story. And why he told it the way he did,
no one will ever know. Lloyd claimed that the group, including
himself, had made it to the top of both peaks! Probably, with all
the hoo-ha surrounding their send-off, he just didn't have the
heart to admit that he, himself, hadn't climbed the mountain.

The headline in W. F. Thompson's *Fairbanks Daily News-
Miner* on April 12 read, "ALASKANS REACH TOP OF SUM-
MIT," and in smaller font underneath, "Tom Lloyd and Party
Reached the Summit of Mount McKinley on April 3 . . . Claim
Cook Did not Reach the Top." The *Fairbanks Daily Times* of
the same day announced the "Proud Boast of Tom Lloyd," that
he had climbed both the South and North Peaks of Mount
McKinley.

Lloyd told his story, which was edited and introduced by W. F. Thompson and printed in the *New York Times Sunday Magazine* on June 5, 1910. By the time the three other members of the party made it to Fairbanks, it was too late; the damage had been done. By then Lloyd had admitted to a few of his friends that he hadn't really made the climb, and the rumors were flying. No matter what Anderson, McGonagall, and Taylor said, no one believed that any of them had made the climb, either.

When asked about Lloyd in his 1937 interview, Billy Taylor said, "He was the head of the party, and we never dreamed he wouldn't give a straight story. I wish to God we hadda been there. Of course our intimate friends believed us."

In 1912 Herschel Parker and Belmore Browne put together another expedition to reach the summit. They were within a few hundred yards of success when horrendous weather conditions forced them to turn back. Although they had looked for the flagpole allegedly planted by what had come to be known as the "Sourdough Expedition," they saw no evidence of it through the storm. This just added fuel to the flame of fabrication.

But the following year another expedition of Alaskans made its assault on the summit. An Episcopal missionary, Hudson Stuck, led a group up the mountain toward the South Peak. Almost to the top, they had stopped to rest at the Grand Basin between the two peaks and were talking about the Sourdough climbers. Suddenly one of the party, Walter Harper, pointed and exclaimed, "I see the flagstaff! I see it plainly!" Harry Karstens, another member of the group, also saw it, and then, using the field glasses, everyone in the party saw and verified the existence of the Sourdoughs' pole. Stuck's party went on up the mountain and entered the record books as the first to make the ascent to the South Peak of Denali, which is 820 feet taller than the North Peak. But now there was no doubt that the Sourdoughs had actually made it to the top, albeit the North Peak top.

So the Sourdough Expedition was vindicated and passed from just hearsay into history. The next expedition to climb the North Peak wasn't until 1932, and by then they found no evidence of the spruce flagstaff.

Until his death in 1940, Dr. Frederick Cook continued to claim he had made the first ascent on Mount McKinley.

Although Tom Lloyd failed to climb to the top of Denali, he still must be given credit for the instigation and planning of the event, and the other three miners given the credit for implementation. These four sourdoughs completed what Hudson Stuck described as "a most extraordinary feat, unique . . . in all the annals of mountaineering."

All in all, it was an accomplishment of mythical proportions, carried out by ordinary men.

CHAPTER 11

The Cache Creek Murders: Who Did It? Where's the Gold?

The year was 1939. It had been a pretty good one for the placer miners seeking gold in the Dutch Hills country west of Talkeetna. The weather hadn't been too bad, except for August. It had rained heavily most of the month, which made mucking around in the creeks and gravel a mess. But it also meant that the creeks held lots of water, which made it easier to wash out their sluice boxes. By September some of the miners had already left the creeks to head out for winter jobs. Their mines had been shut down and equipment stored for next year. Some of the miners, however, were planning to work on into October, hoping to extract just a little bit more pay dirt before hard winter set in.

But in the second week of September happenings of such brutality occurred in the Dutch Hills that mining came to a quick standstill. Four members of the community lost their lives in savage, vicious attacks on the same day.

There was quite a compatible group of miners in the neighborhood, many of whom had worked in the area for several years. Since one never knew who would suddenly be in need of help, everyone was always ready to pitch in if a neighbor were in trouble. The spirit of cooperation had been around since the "old days," back when Susitna Station was the supply center for the miners and trappers working in the valley.

In 1916 Talkeetna was the work camp for the crews building the railroad. At first the bulk of the population consisted of railroad workers, but soon small businesses began to appear. H. W. Nagley's small supply station moved from Susitna and became a well-stocked general store. There was a bakery and a bunkhouse.

A road was built out to the Cache Creek gold claims, which made access to the Dutch and Peters Hills easier also. As word got out that there was gold in the hills, and the access improved, a few more miners came into the area each year. By the mid-1930s, there were about four dozen residents in Talkeetna. About half of those were miners who spent their summers on their claims and winters in town. Many miners worked trap lines in the winter to make enough money from furs to do mining in the summer. These fellows would appear in town for a few days in the winter, then head back out to their traps.

The grisly story begins with Frank Jenkins, who came to Alaska from California in 1902 when he was twenty-three years old. By 1916 he had moved to the new town of Talkeetna and become active in the community there. He had claims or parts of

THOMAS CULHANE PAPERS, ARCHIVES AND SPECIAL
COLLECTIONS, CONSORTIUM LIBRARY, UNIVERSITY
OF ALASKA ANCHORAGE

Placer mining on Willow Creek summer of 1939

claims in several locations in the Dutch and Peters Hills, but his primary holdings were placer claims along Little Willow Creek. By fall of 1923, Frank was forty-four years old. He had married, and his wife, Helen, ten years younger than he, was small and petite with an argumentative personality.

Frank and Helen's claims were very productive, and it was often noted in the newspapers at the end of the season that "the Jenkins' holdings did well." By 1930, Helen and Frank had a nice cabin on Little Willow Creek. They also had holdings on Willow Creek, which Little Willow Creek joined.

South of the Jenkinses' workings farther down the creek were several claims that belonged to Christ Hansen. He had been mining in the area for many more years than had Jenkins, and he was concerned that Frank Jenkins's operations were beginning to have some impact on his own. In placer mining, gravel that may contain gold is washed and rewashed with water rushing over it as it is pushed along troughs, called sluice boxes. The water washes over ridges that are designed to catch the heavier gold, as the gravel is washed down and out of the sluice boxes. The gravel debris that is washed down into the creeks below the operation is referred to as the "tailings."

Jenkins's tailings were being washed downstream into Hansen's mining area. Hansen asserted that he had tried to discuss the tailings with the Jenkinses, but they wouldn't listen to him. Finally Hansen became so upset that he took them to court over it. The legal action continued on through the fall and into the winter. Hansen's lawyer would file, and the Jenkinses' lawyer would file back, all of these filings requiring the attendance in Anchorage by the opposing parties. Finally the case was brought to trial without a jury in March of 1931, and, much to Hansen's consternation, the judge granted the Jenkinses' lawyers request for dismissal on "grounds of insufficient proof."

Dick Francis had also come to Alaska from California. He was thirty-four years old when he left Seattle in 1913 for the far north. After traveling about Alaska for a bit, he zeroed in on the Talkeetna area and staked some claims on Long Creek that flowed north out of the Peters Hills toward the Tokositna River.

In 1919 Francis was in Anchorage, got into a fight, and broke his left arm. He was angry enough to take his assailant to court. It is unknown how the case turned out, but it does indicate that Francis, like Jenkins, had a penchant for litigation.

Francis continued to work his holdings on Long Creek for several years. Then he decided to branch out, and in 1932 and 1933 he staked several claims on Ruby Creek, which flowed into Willow.

Frank Jenkins watched the Ruby Creek mining with trepidation. He actually hired two other miners working up on Ruby Creek to "keep an eye" on the work that Francis was doing there. The previous summer Jenkins had had a conflict with another miner whom he thought was working too close to his claims, and had intimidated the miner into moving his operations to a different place. Helen was even more suspicious than her husband and frequently voiced her dislike for and distrust of Francis and his Ruby Creek digs.

Frank Jenkins became increasingly upset at the way Dick Francis was mining Ruby Creek. Jenkins insisted that the debris washing down from Ruby was ruining his own claims on Willow Creek. This concern led to another court suit. The hearing was supposed to be in Seward, but Francis's lawyer was able to move it to Anchorage so that his client would not have to leave his trapping line and suffer financial loss. The arguments persisted through the following winter of 1935, with both Jenkins and Francis having lawyers pitted against one another. Francis was ordered by the court to build a box that would catch the debris before it reached Jenkins's works, but Jenkins was not satisfied with the way the operation was handled. On more than one occasion there was conflict over who had staked which claim on Willow or Ruby Creek. As time went on, hard feelings grew between the two men. Helen also grew more pointedly suspicious of their neighbor.

Over the next few years Jenkins and Francis had several more litigious encounters. Helen was particularly vocal about her dislike of Francis, even saying that she would like to go burn down his cabin. Francis grew more bitter also, and he uttered threats against the couple.

The Jenkinses worked hard, and although they were well-known in the area, they kept to themselves. It was reputed that the gold recovered from their mining efforts was considerable, and that Frank cached it in different spots around his property, as he did not trust banks. He had lost money in a bank that failed in the "crash of '29."

As the Jenkinses' placer mining operations expanded, they hired more workers. Two of the workers, brothers Ken and Joy Brittell, got along very well with them. In 1939 Joy, Ken and his new wife, Maxine, and her brother, Tim Craig, worked their own claim near Ramsdyke Gulch on Wolf Creek, over the ridge from Dick Francis's camp. They often visited back and forth with the Jenkinses, who were happy to give them advice. During one visit, Helen Jenkins showed Maxine six small bags of gold, each sorted according to "nugget size," which she was keeping in a large black purse. She told Maxine good places to hide gold were "under the woodpile" or "in your flour bag." She reiterated her husband's distrust of banks and his habit of hiding small pokes of gold around until he could add them to the main cache that he would take out of the area at the end of each summer.

That summer of 1939 brought another newcomer to the close-knit mining community. In March, a stranger came by train from Anchorage. He was described as having cold, gray-blue eyes and a pasty complexion, with a scar around his neck, just under his chin. He gave his name as Xan John Clarke, called himself John, and took lodging at the Talkeetna Trading Post. He was a Canadian who had come to the United States and joined the US Army. He served for nine years and applied for American citizenship before he left the service. He had come to Alaska the year before and done a little prospecting, then worked for a coal company in the Matanuska Valley. He had injured his back in an accident at the mine and after his recovery had come to prospect in Cache Creek country.

Clarke was a sociable person and liked to chat. He asked a lot of questions about gold mining and was especially interested in knowing who the most successful miners were and where they mined. He started out prospecting before the snow had melted, and at one time broke into an old cabin in one of Frank Jenkins's old camps. He told Jenkins that he had had to break in because of bad weather. Frank said that if nothing was taken and Clarke replaced the lock, there was no problem. Helen, though, wanted to prosecute him.

After a few weeks Clarke staked some claims on Ramsdyke Gulch and moved into an abandoned cabin there. Although he did a little prospecting, he seemed mostly to be prospecting for information. He spent a lot of time traveling to visit with different miners and would often arrive about dinnertime, where the code of the creeks dictated that he would be invited for a meal and some conversation. He became well aware of the bad blood between Jenkins and Francis and wasted no words in exploiting it. He was not above repeating to Francis what Helen threatened to do to him or to the Jenkinses what wild threats Francis threw around toward them.

Clarke was extremely interested in how much gold the Jenkinses might get from their operations each summer, and, was it true that Frank hid it somewhere around the camp? The miners he questioned usually just changed the subject or told him bluntly that it wasn't any of their business. He had specifically asked the Brittell brothers, since they had worked for Jenkins. Ken said he should ask Frank Jenkins if he really wanted to know!

Probably he did not ask Frank, but he did spend a lot of time at the Jenkins cabin. He often visited once or twice a week.

Then came rainy August, and after four weeks of profitable mining in uncomfortable weather, the season was winding down. Ken and Maxine Brittell, and Maxine's brother, Tim Craig, had packed up and started their walk out to Talkeetna early, on August 23. They couldn't carry their heavy radio and its even heavier battery in their packs; they left it with Joy who would send it to them when they reached Unga Island on the Alaska Peninsula where Ken had a teaching job.

The three hikers took it slow with their heavy packs and made it to the Jenkinses' camp where they planned to spend the first night.

Frank and Helen talked about their summer and indicated that it had been their best one yet, having mined several thousand dollars. Helen even showed them some large nuggets from their workings.

Joy Brittell stayed behind and spent several days closing down their camp. He stored the radio and battery at John Clarke's cabin until he could retrieve it for Ken and Maxine. He then moved to the Jenkinses' where he had agreed to stay and work for them until they closed down their operation in October. Bob Meade, a young man who had been hired by Jenkins to fill in for an injured worker, would be working there into September for a week or two as well.

On September 6, Jenkins, Joy Brittell, and Bob Meade were eating lunch when John Clarke showed up at the cabin. The three workers went on out to work, and Helen offered Clarke some lunch. He not only had lunch, but also hung around all afternoon and was still there when the men returned for dinner.

After dinner, Jenkins turned on the radio to listen to the news. After the news, the radio station had a "bush line," where messages could be sent out to anyone in listening distance. That night there was a message for Joy, that Ken and Maxine were leaving Seward the next day for Squaw Harbor, and Joy could send the radio any time.

The next day, the rain moved back in, and the Jenkins crew worked feverishly to get the last of the gold out of the riffles.

By September 9, the last cleanup of the sluice boxes produced a goodly amount of gold and Frank Jenkins finished his best gold mining season ever. Bob Meade made his preparations to leave the next morning. Because the weather was clearing again, Frank Jenkins and Joy Brittell decided to go the next day to get the radio and battery from John Clarke's cabin.

Early the next day, a Sunday, Bob Meade left with his pack to walk out to Talkeetna. Later in the morning, Frank and Joy shouldered their empty packboards and started over the steep ridge to the trail that led to Ramsdyke Gulch where John Clarke's cabin held Ken and Maxine's radio and battery.

The weather remained clear all that day and was clear again on Monday. Early that morning John Clarke walked by Dick Francis's cabin and called a "hello." When Dick failed to answer, Clarke looked in the window and saw Dick lying dead on the floor, with a pool of blood at his head and a pistol in his hand. Then, according to Clarke, he walked over to tell the Jenkinses, but no one was there.

By evening the word had reached Petersville, where there was a plane. The pilot flew to Talkeetna and alerted the commissioner, Ben Mayfield. He contacted the US attorney, Joseph Kehoe, in Seward and explained the situation. Kehoe told Mayfield to get out to the Dutch Hills as soon as he could, and when the weather allowed, Kehoe would come to Talkeetna to assist.

At first, because of the widely known bad feelings between the two camps, it was thought that Francis had murdered the Jenkinses and then shot himself. But then Clarke told Mayfield that Joy Brittell was working for Jenkins and was probably also missing. He noted that the radio and battery were gone from his cabin and assumed that the two men had been there on Sunday while he was visiting Francis. Mayfield organized a search party for the two men, starting up over the ridge from Clarke's cabin.

It was not until Thursday, September 14, that the search party discovered the bodies of the two missing men, covered with grass. Frank Jenkins's head was crushed and his throat cut "from ear to ear." Joy Brittell's throat was cut and his head also badly cut and bruised.

But where was Helen?

Four days later, on September 18, Frank Lee found Helen Jenkins's body. Frank had been thinking about where Helen would likely have walked if she were looking for her husband, and searched very slowly along the trail by the creek. Her body was carefully hidden under the edge of the creek bank not too far from the camp. The commission report stated, "It appeared she had been hacked with an ax." All of her pockets were turned inside out, so robbery was assumed to be the motive.

The original theory that Francis had killed Jenkins and then shot himself was deemed invalid when it was discovered that Dick Francis had been shot twice, not once, in the head, so he couldn't have shot himself. Also, the gun was found in his right hand, and the two bullets had entered on the left side of his head.

So now the miners began to talk among themselves. They couldn't believe that there would be any one of them that could commit such heinous crimes. They also didn't really believe that an unknown maniac murderer was on the loose. So they focused on the stranger, John Clarke. It was remembered that he was the one who discovered the first body. And he was also with the searchers when they found the bodies of Jenkins and Brittell. It was thought that Helen had gone out to look for Frank and Joy when they hadn't returned from getting the radios. Clarke could have killed her, taken her keys to get into the cabin, and ransacked it looking for gold, then left the keys inside and relocked the door.

The Anchorage papers carried headlines for weeks about the murders. It was the newspaper that first referred to them as the "Cache Creek Murders." There was outrage that the killer had not been found and brought to justice. There was outrage that there were no federal lawmen in all of Alaska. There were letters sent to J. Edgar Hoover.

An editorial in the *Anchorage Daily Times,* entitled "Shameful Indifference" read, in part:

> Two weeks have gone since the quadruple slayings came to light. About 150 persons in the Cache Creek country are living under most tense circumstances. Many are packing weapons for fear of attack. What is being done about the massacre? Where are the law enforcement agencies of the territory and of the United States?

So the FBI sent agent R. C. Vogel to Talkeetna. Commissioner Mayfield filled him in on all the details. Vogel spent several weeks interviewing all of the miners in the area, especially those who lived near the cabins of either Francis or the Jenkinses. With Mayfield, he went over and over the testimonies of everyone connected with the case in any way, especially John Clarke. There were many suspicions regarding Clarke's actions before and after the murders. Vogel uncovered the story that Clarke had prospected the year before in the Nelchina mining district near Palmer with two other miners. Clarke and one of the miners had returned to Anchorage after the mining season, but the other miner had not been seen nor heard from again.

On October 6 John Clarke sold his Ramsdyke Gulch claims. On October 7 he sailed from Seward to Seattle, where his wife was awaiting his arrival. Several people noted that he was carrying a large duffle bag when he boarded the train in Talkeetna. Agent Vogel was in Seward to confer with Joseph Kehoe and noticed Clarke's name on the roster of passengers sailing to Seattle, so he booked passage on the same ship. He interviewed Clarke again in transit.

In November, FBI Agent E. M. O'Donnell arrived in Anchorage to help out with the investigation. O'Donnell went over all of the testimonies previously given and examined all the evidence, traveling from Anchorage to Talkeetna, and even Fairbanks. Vogel continued to examine evidence also.

The caretaker hired to oversee the Jenkinses' camp until Frank's brother could come to take care of it found $5,000 worth of gold in small bags hidden under the woodpile. Rumors continued to float that the Jenkinses had much more gold than that found hidden away. Robbery continued to be thought the motive for the murders.

Tips continued to come in from all over Alaska about strangers who "looked suspicious" and had "lots of money." All of the tips were explored, without success.

In March of 1940 an agent interviewed John Clarke again in Seattle. In July FBI Special Agent J. D. Noble arrived in Anchorage to begin a new investigation. Vogel was still going over evidence in Juneau.

In January 1941, another agent questioned Clarke in Seattle. In February Clarke wrote to J. Edgar Hoover complaining about harassment and asking that all the property that had been taken from him as evidence be returned.

On December 7, 1941, Japan bombed Pearl Harbor. The FBI was immediately busy on all fronts with national security. No more reports about the Cache Creek murders were filed with them until May 14, 1942.

Then on July 7, 1943, a report was filed in Juneau that began:

A review of the file reflects that in all probability Richard A. Francis, carried as one of the victims, murdered the other three victims and then committed suicide.

At the end of the file the status of the case was marked CLOSED. That status was never made public.

And so the Cache Creek murders remain, in the minds of those who still remember them, unsolved. It was the consensus of all involved in the case that it was unlikely, even impossible, that Dick Francis had killed the other three and taken his own life. It was heavily believed that John Clarke was the culprit. It is still speculated that there is gold hidden somewhere around the Jenkinses' Willow Creek holdings.

John Clarke died in 1971, with the case still unresolved.

Dennis Garrett worked the deserted Willow Creek and Ruby Creek claims in the 1980s and 1990s. There is an old trail through the brush leading to what was Frank Jenkins's cabin. The first time Garrett walked the trail, he felt a strong wave of fear wash over him, and the hair on his head stood on end.

Whose ghost is haunting that trail? Is it one of the victims, or the killer revisiting the scenes of his crime?

CHAPTER 12

The Mysterious Flight of JAL 1628

The Alaska winter night sky is full of spectacular lights. The blanket of stars that stretches from horizon to horizon shines and reflects on the snow below, and moonlight creates an illusion of bright daytime on a cloudless night. When the aurora borealis dances across the northern sky, the shimmering sheets of reds, yellows, and greens excite the minds and gladden the hearts of those who see the glorious sight. Regularly scheduled airline flights and many private airplanes zip back and forth across the sky, visible to those below by their identifying signal lights.

But on the night of November 17, 1986, were there other lights in the Alaska night sky?

On that day, about 5:00 p.m., Japan Air Lines Flight 1628 flew into the Alaska sky. A 747, JAL 1628 was a cargo plane, and it had started out the day before from Paris, France, carrying a load of wine to be delivered to Japan. On board were Captain Kenju Terauchi, Takanori Tamefuji, the copilot, and Yoshio Tsukuda, the engineer. After a stopover in Reykjavik, Iceland, the flight had continued west, where it would finish the first leg of the journey in Anchorage. There the three-man crew would be relieved. There was a faint afterglow of sunset on the western horizon as they flew over Edmonton and crossed the Canada–Alaska border.

At 5:09 p.m. local Alaska Time, the Anchorage Air Route Traffic Control Center (AARTCC) communicated with JAL 1628 to report they had initial radar contact and asked the captain to turn slightly left toward Talkeetna. This would send them south of Fort Yukon and Fairbanks. As Captain Terauchi banked to the left, he noticed lights slightly to the left and below his line of flight. He assumed that they were some sort of military aircraft from Eielson or Elmendorf Air Force Base, part of the continued surveillance over Alaska in those years, because of being near the Soviet Union, so he ignored them.

A couple of minutes later, the captain realized that the lights were traveling in the same direction and at the same speed as his plane. After about seven minutes of flying next to them, the lights suddenly appeared in front of the plane where they were observed through the left front window at approximately the "eleven o'clock" position. Captain Terauchi reported later that "most unexpectedly, two spaceships stopped in front of our face, shooting off lights. The inside cockpit shined brightly, and I felt warm in the face." The two "ships" appeared to be flying one directly over the other.

At this point, about 5:19 p.m., the crew decided to try to find out what they were seeing. Copilot Tamefuji called the AARTCC on the radio. "Do you have any traffic in front of us?" he asked.

Then commenced several back and forth communications in which the AARTCC asked if JAL could identify the traffic, or if they could describe it. JAL reported that they could not identify it, nor tell if it were military or civilian. The crew could see navigation and strobe lights, which they described as white and yellow. Later when the crew was interviewed with a translator, they also mentioned green.

The Anchorage Control Center asked for a description of flying conditions, that is, if conditions were normal or if there were clouds below the craft, for example. The copilot confirmed that conditions were normal, and that there were thin and spotty clouds near the mountains. At this time the radio transmissions became somewhat garbled, as if there were interference on the frequencies. In later interviews Captain Terauchi remembered that communication with Anchorage was difficult for ten to fifteen minutes while the little mystery ships were close, then became better as they left.

The two ships that had appeared to be flying one above the other changed positions, so they were now flying side by side. Then they suddenly moved away.

About four minutes after their first inquiry, JAL 1628 reported, "And now the target, ah, traffic is extinguished. We cannot see it now."

Anchorage answered, "JAL 1628 Roger. And I'm not receiving any radar replies."

Subsequently, as Captain Terauchi looked to the left, he saw what he described as a "flat pale white light," larger than the two smaller "ships." It looked to him as if the two smaller white lights had traveled toward the larger light. He wasn't sure if the two white lights had become the larger pale light, or if the pale light was something completely different. The copilot and engineer could not clearly see the larger light through the left window, so they could not describe its shape at that time, but they did concur that there were lights in that direction.

Although the ground radar had not detected any object, Captain Terauchi checked his digital weather radar in the 747, and there on the screen was a round green "blip" about seven or eight miles away in the direction of the large light. He asked Anchorage if they saw anything on the ground radar at that time.

Excitedly, Anchorage answered, "Heavy, [a term used when speaking to, or about, the largest class of aircraft, such as a 747] roger, sir. I'm picking up a hit on the radar approximately five miles in trail of your six o'clock position [i.e., behind the plane]."

By this time Anchorage had contacted the Air Force at Elmendorf Regional Operational Control Center (ROCC) to see if they had anything on their radar besides the JAL 1628 747.

After spending a couple of minutes looking, the Elmendorf ROCC reported that they were getting some "surge primary return."

Each commercial (and military) airplane is assigned a unique transponder code in order to automatically identify it on radar. A transponder is "a device for receiving a radio signal and automatically transmitting a different signal." On a radar screen, any identifiable aircraft appears as a transponder return, with two side-by-side blips on the screen. Any aircraft without a transponder appears as one blip, and is referred to as a "primary return."

Anchorage asked Elmendorf to verify if there were any military aircraft aloft in the area. Elmendorf reported no aircraft aloft and asked Anchorage to provide the location of the primary return they were receiving. Anchorage placed it now right in front of JAL 1628.

Elmendorf responded, "OK. I've got him about his, ah, oh, it looks like about, ah, ten o'clock at about that range." It seemed that now ROTCC could also see the accompanying "traffic."

Shortly after that exchange the primary returns disappeared from both Anchorage and Elmendorf radar screens.

At some point during this time, Captain Terauchi asked Tsukuda for his camera bag, which was behind the captain and beside the engineer. For several minutes Terauchi attempted to photograph the lights on the two little ships that he could see out in front of the 747. Unfortunately, he had difficulty with the operation of the camera and couldn't get it to hold a focus, so he put it away in order to concentrate on the "traffic" accompanying them. He later commented that it was a new camera, and he hadn't used it before.

By now, JAL 1628 was nearing Fairbanks. Up until then, the lighter part of the sky was on the right of the plane, with the left being dark except for the pale lights to the side. As they flew above the city lights, however, Captain Terauchi looked out at the pale lights and was able to see, silhouetted against the lighter sky now, a gigantic spaceship! Anxious to avoid it, and a bit unnerved, he requested to Anchorage a change of course.

About 5:30 p.m. JAL 1628 called Anchorage, "Request deviate from object request heading two four zero."

Anchorage replied, "Roger. Fly heading two four zero. Deviations approved as necessary for traffic."

JAL 1628 reported, "It's, ah, quite big . . ."

Anchorage, "Say again."

JAL 1628, "It's, ah, very quite big, ah, plane."

After JAL 1628 made the forty-five-degree right turn, the large ship was still following it. The captain then requested and was given permission for a 360-degree turn, also to descend from thirty-five thousand feet to thirty-one thousand feet.

After those maneuvers were complete, Anchorage asked JAL 1628 if it still had its "traffic." They replied, "Still, ah, coming, right in formation."

Five minutes later JAL copilot Tamefuji requested permission to proceed directly to the Talkeetna checkpoint. Anchorage agreed and then decided to test the "traffic" by having JAL 1628 make another 360-degree turn and advise how the "traffic" behaved. As Captain Terauchi made the turn, he reported that the "traffic" had disappeared.

Then Elmendorf was heard from again.

"On some other equipment here we have confirmed there is a flight size of two around. One primary return only."

Anchorage, "OK. Where is, is he following him?"

Elmendorf, "It looks like he is, yes."

Anchorage, "OK. Stand by."

Anchorage contacted JAL 1628 and relayed the information that military radar indicated a primary return behind the 747. A few minutes later Elmendorf reported that he had lost sight of the primary return. Eleven seconds later JAL 1628 reported, "We have in sight same position." The 747 was just coming out of its 360-degree turn and heading straight now toward Talkeetna. It appeared as if the giant spaceship had dropped back until the turn was completed then resumed its position to the left of the plane.

At 5:53 p.m., JAL 1628 made its final report regarding its flying companion.

"Maintaining flight level two five zero, so, I cannot, I couldn't see, UFO, over."

Anchorage, "Understand. You do not see the traffic any longer."

JAL 1628, "Affirmative."

The "incident" had lasted forty-four minutes.

No doubt all involved were immensely relieved when the wine-laden 747 finally landed at Anchorage Airport.

Because of the unusual traffic reported by the flight, all three crew members were interviewed after their arrival in Anchorage. FAA Official Jack Wright and Special Agents James Derry and Ronald Mickle conducted the interviews. The JAL operations manager in Anchorage, Mr. Shibashi also joined them. All three of the JAL 1628 crew members verified the sightings and described them in primarily the same way. Captain Terauchi described some of the lights that the other two had sensed, but could not see as well, since the lights were on the opposite side of the plane from where they sat. Unfortunately, the interviewers did not record their conversations, but agents Derry and Mickle did take notes. Captain Terauchi drew some diagrams showing

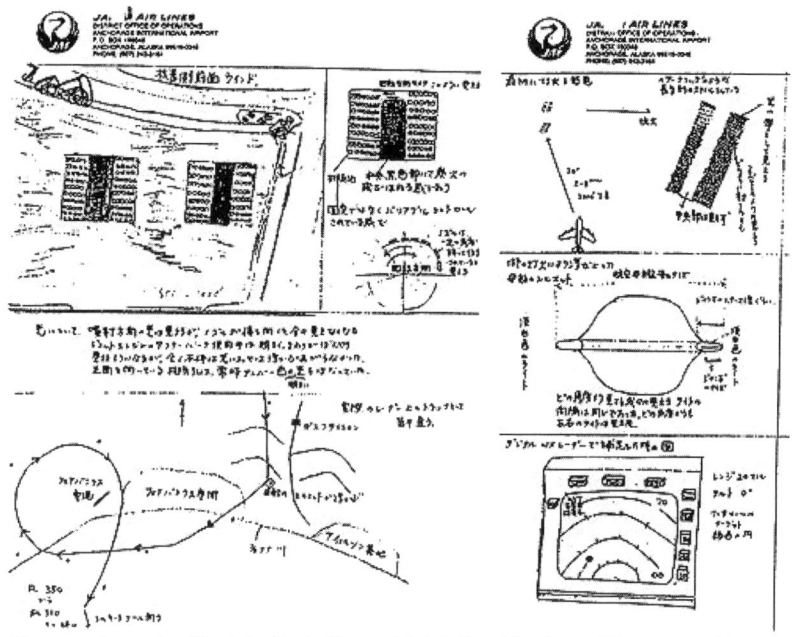

Diagram drawn by Captain Kenju Terauchi detailing his view of the spaceship

Courtesy of the Federal Aviation Administration (FAA)

where the lights appeared to them, both when in front and when beside their aircraft. The next day the air traffic controller who had communicated with JAL 1628 throughout their harrowing ordeal wrote down all that he remembered of the conversations.

Agent Derry did ask if the air force were keeping the data on the flight and was assured in the affirmative. Mr. Wright communicated his information to the FAA Security Office in Washington, DC, but apparently no action regarding the report was taken at that time, and investigation into the sightings went no further.

It was not until more than a month later that the story about the Japanese plane and the UFO began to surface. It seems that rumors began to fly as the crew of JAL 1628 talked to their friends and colleagues about their amazing adventure.

On Christmas Eve the public information officer in Anchorage, Paul Steucke, was contacted by the Kyoda News Service in Japan. They sent someone to interview him about the events reported by the crew of JAL 1628. Steucke told them about the air traffic controller tapes and the subsequent interviews with the crew. The story was apparently printed in Japan, United Press International repeated it, and it went on from there.

On December 29 the story broke in the US papers and the fun began. The FAA press office in Alaska contacted John J. Callahan, the division chief of the Accidents, Evaluations and Investigations of the FAA in Washington, DC, and wanted to know what they should tell the press when asked about the UFO sightings.

"Tell them we are 'investigating' them," was Callahan's response.

Washington contacted Anchorage Air Traffic Control and was pleased to discover that the tapes had been saved, instead of being reused after thirty days, which was the usual procedure.

So, the FAA reopened their investigation by interviewing Captain Terauchi on January 2, 1987. There he gave written testimony and also drew diagrams of what he had seen. He drew the outline that he had seen of the large object that had appeared on the left of the plane, and which he referred to as the "Mother Ship." He compared its size to "two aircraft carriers." That same day, Larry King interviewed Captain Terauchi on US television. For several days thereafter Terauchi became quite a celebrity, appearing on several radio and television programs. He continued to stand by his observations and explained his diagrams to the American public through translators.

Both of the other crew members, Takanori Tamefuji and Yoshio Tsukuda, were also interviewed extensively. Although they did not claim to see all of the details observed by Kenju Terauchi because they were seated on the other side of the plane, they did verify the first lights seen through the front windows as small spaceships and agreed that there was a larger pale light down to the left and in the pilot's view.

As the FAA continued its investigation, explanations for the reported events continued to be offered. The Committee for Scientific Investigation of Claims of the Paranormal (CSI-COP) reported "UFO Mystery Solved," by announcing that the sightings were probably the planet Jupiter, and possibly also the planet Mars. This was because those two "extraterrestrial objects" were exceptionally bright at that time, with Mars being slightly below Jupiter. (The following summer the CSICOP recanted that explanation and replaced it with "reflections of moonlight from thin clouds and 'turbulent ice crystals' above them.")

The January 26, 1987, edition of *People* magazine reported the incident with a tone of sarcasm, with the headline, "Through the Alaskan Darkness Kenju Terauchi, a 747 Pilot, Is Pursued by a UFO—Or So He Claims." The article is captivatingly written, and although it doesn't discount any of Terauchi's account of the UFO event, it does state that the truth hinges on the captain's believability.

Then on March 6, 1987, the *Anchorage Daily News,* on page one, reported from the FAA press release, "FAA Has No Conclusion about UFO." According to the article, the FAA had reviewed the first-person testimony of each of the JAL crew members, read and re-read the statements from the radio controllers and gone through "reams of radar data." The agency spokesman, Paul Steucke, stated, "The FAA does not have enough material to say that something was there. We are accepting the descriptions of the crew but are unable to support what they saw."

The article went on to explain that the ground radar controllers had misinterpreted a "split image" of JAL 1628 as a second object without a transponder.

And with that, the FAA investigation of the JAL 1628's experience with a UFO over Alaska was complete.

John J. Callahan was involved in the investigation on every front. When the FAA turned it over to President Reagan's scientific staff, consisting of the CIA and the president's science advisors, he went over all of the data with them. When all of their questions had been addressed, Callahan asked one of the CIA persons what he thought it was. The person answered that it was a UFO, but went on to say that if the American public were told there was a UFO, they would panic, so "this event never happened."

The FAA took boxes and boxes of info that they had shared and stored them. Eventually the final FAA report was brought back to Callahan's office, where it, along with the voice tapes of the incident and the chart produced at the Tech Center, sat on a table in a corner waiting for the CIA to come and get them. They were still there when he retired from his position in 1988. The incoming office manager packed up everything in the office, including the papers on the table, and shipped them to Callahan's home, where they remained.

The official explanation of this "non-event" remains that it was the result of a "split-image" on the radar screen, or a "hardware" or "software" problem. But more than twenty years later, Callahan holds to the UFO theory. He believes the crew members reported true sightings, and that the radar corroborated them.

So the big question remains. On November 17, 1986, was there a huge "Mothership" exploring Alaska airspace, releasing two small ships to reconnoiter the Japan Air Line 747? What did the ground radar really show?

Incidentally, on January 29, 1987, an Alaska Airlines flight reported a fast moving unidentified object on their weather radar on a flight from Nome to Anchorage. It was out of range of the ARTCC so could not be verified. On January 30 of the same year, a US Air Force jet reported a large, disc-shaped object when they were flying from Anchorage to Fairbanks. It quickly disappeared from sight.

BIBLIOGRAPHY

Kah Lituya Strikes!

Caldwell, Francis E. *Land of the Ocean Mists.* Annapolis: Lighthouse Press, 2003, 1960.

Fradkin, Philip L. *Wildest Alaska.* Berkeley: University of California Press, 2001.

Miller, Donald J. *Giant Waves in Lituya Bay, Alaska.* USGA Professional Paper 354-C. Washington, DC: US Government Printing Office.

Schooler, Lynn. *Walking Home.* New York: Bloomsbury USA, 2010.

Baychimo, Phantom of the Arctic

Bolton, Alan. www.btinternet.com/~alan.bolton/hbc_main .html.

Boswell, Randy. "Reappearing Ghost." *The Vancouver Sun.* Thursday, May 4, 2006.

Dalton, Anthony. *Baychimo: Arctic Ghost Ship.* Victoria: Heritage House Publishing Company, Ltd., 2006.

Hoyle, Gwyneth. *Flowers in the Snow: The Life of Isobel Wylie Hutchison.* Lincoln: University of Nebraska Press, 2001.

Hutchison, Isobel Wylie. *North to the Rime-ringed Sun: Being the Record of an Alaskan-Canadian Journey Made in 1933–34.* London: Blackie and Son Limited, 1934.

Jamieson, A. J. *The Last Voyage of the Baychimo.* www.theoutlaws .com/ unexplained8b.htm.

GHOSTLY RESCUES

Berton, Pierre. *Klondike Fever—The Life and Death of the Last Great Gold Rush.* New York: Carroll & Graf Publishers, 1958.

Ferrell, Ed. *Strange Stories of Alaska and the Yukon.* Fairbanks: Epicenter Press, 1996.

Harrison, Edward Sanford. *Nome and Seward Peninsula: history, description, biographies and stories.* Seattle: The Metropolitan Press, 1905.

Newell, Gordon R. ed. *H.W. McCurdy Marine History of the Pacific Northwest.* Seattle: Superior Publishing, 1966.

Tillion, Clem. Telephone interview with author, August 2011.

Tillion, Diana. "John." *Alaska Voices, Voices from Kachemak Bay.* Homer: Disk Makers, 2005.

THE HAIRY MAN

Alley, J. Robert. *Raincoast Sasquatch.* Surrey, British Columbia: Hancock House Publishers, 2003.

Christian, Greg. Telephone interview with author, April 7, 2012.

Josephs, Brad. Telephone interview with author, March 9, 2012.

Klouda, Naomi. "Port Chatham left to spirits." *Homer Tribune,* October 11, 2009.

Schlief, Ed. Telephone interview with author, April 4, 2012.

Sherwonit, Bill. *Travelers' Tales Alaska.* San Francisco: Travelers' Tales, Inc., 2003.

WHAT IS UNDER THE WATER?

Bille, Matt. "What Lies Beneath Lake Iliamna?" Alaska Science Outreach, October 24, 2004. www.alaskascienceoutreach. com/index.php/features/sis_parttwo/what-lies-beneath-lake-iliamna.

Coleman, Loren. "Sea Serpents Likely to be Discovered." High Strangeness, Signs of the Times. sott.net. www.sott.net/articles/show/179904-Sea-Serpents-Likely-to-be-Discovered.

Compton, James R. "Slick, Thomas Baker, Jr.," Texas State Historical Association. www.tshaonline.org/handbook/online/articles/fs107.

Dunham, Mike. "Rare reptile fossil found in Southeast." *Anchorage Daily News,* Thursday, July 28, 2011: A-4.

"Iliamna Lake Monster." Unknown Explorers. www .unknownexplorers.com/iliamnalakemonsters.php.

Levy, Dianne. "Jason Seabury." The Maritime Heritage Project, San Francisco. D. Blethen Adams Levy. www. maritimeheritage.org/captains/jasonSeabury.htm.

Speigel, Lee. "Alaska's Loch Ness Monster Is Latest Alleged Sea Serpent Sighting." Huffington Post. www.huffingtonpost. com/2011/07/20/alaska-loch-ness-monster_n_904658.html.

Toombs, Terry. "Alaska folklore: Five mythical creatures of the Last Frontier." Alaska Dispatch News and Views from the Last Frontier, June 12, 2012. www.alaskadispatch.com/ article/alaska-folklore-five-mythical-creatures-last-frontier.

Van Lanen, James. "Iliamna Lake Seals Local and Scientific Understanding." Alaska Fish & Wildlife News. Alaska Department of Fish & Game July 2012. www.adfg.alaska. gov/index.cfm?adfg=wildlifenews.view_articles&articles_ id=553.

"White Sturgeon." Pacific States Marine Fisheries Commission. www.psmfc.org/habitat/edu_wsturg_fact.html.

Wright, Bruce. "Scientist wonders if Nessie-like monster in Alaska lake is a sleeper shark." Alaska Dispatch News and Views from the Last Frontier, May 3, 2012. www

.alaskadispatch.com/article/scientist-wonders-if-nessie-
monster-alaska-lake-sleeper-shark.

THE "LITTLE PEOPLE" OF THE ARCTIC

Dunham, Mike. "'Little people' e-mail zips through rural
Alaska." *Anchorage Daily News,* June 1, 2008. http://and
.com/2008/05/31.v-printer/422883/little-people-e-mail-zips-
through.html.

Fienup-Riordan, Ann. *Boundaries and Passages: Rule and Ritual
in Yup'ik Eskimo Oral Tradition.* Norman: University of
Oklahoma Press, 1995.

————. *Things of Our Ancestors: Yup'ik Elders Explore the
Jacobsen Collection at the Ethnologisches Museum Berlin.*
Seattle: University of Washington, 2005.

————. *Wise Words of the Yup'ik People: We Talk to You Because
We Love You.* Lincoln: University of Nebraska Press, 2005.

Graham, Douglas D. "The Alaska X-Files." *Alaska Magazine,*
October 1999: 41, 42.

Imaje, Majik. "The Enukins—Little People of NW Alaska (Pt,
Hope) as told by an Inupiaq man, Bigfoot Encounters. www.
bigfootencounters.com/creatures/enukins.htm.

Institute of Social and Economic Research, University of
Alaska. www.Alaskool.org. www.alaskool.org/projects/chevak/
chevak/John's_stories.html.

Kolausok, Eddie Dean. "The Last Visit by the Little People." PROVENANCE.ca for librarians, archivists & professional preservers-creators of information ISSN 1203-8954 Canada .www.provenance .ca/2004-vol6/column-arctic-canada/book-call-me-ishmael .html.

"Little People of the Tundra." Yupik Indian Folklore. Native Languages of the Americas: Yupik Indian Legends. www .native-languages.org.yupik-legends.htm.

THE ICE WORM COMETH

DeArmond, R. N. *Klondike Newsman "Stroller" White.* Skagway: Lynn Canal Publishing, 1990.

Glacier Ranger District, Chugach National Forest, Alaska Geographic [brochure], 2008.

Service, Robert. *Bar-Room Ballads.* New York: Dodd Mead 1940.

Shain, Daniel H. *Annelids in Modern Biology.* Hoboken: Wiley-Blackwell, 2009.

———. E-mail correspondence with author, May 2012.

Willoughby, Barrett. *Alaskans All.* Boston and New York: Houghton Mifflin, 1933.

PERMAFROST—INTO THE ICE AGE, AND BEFORE

Abbott, Alison. "Palaeontology: Tunnel Vision." *Nature International Weekly Journal of Science October 31 2007.* www .nature.com/news/2007/07/071031/full/450018a.html.

Gangloff, Roland A. *Dinosaurs under the Aurora.* Indianapolis: University of Indiana Press, 2012.

Hennessey, Julia. "Does Permafrost Affect Trees?" eHow. www .ehow.com/print/how-does-4914860_does-permafrost-affect-trees.html.

Seifert, Richard. "Permafrost: A Building Problem in Alaska." *The University of Alaska Fairbanks Cooperative Extension Service:* Reprinted September 2011.

Selinger, Gary. "Blue Babe, A Messenger from the Ice Age." *UA Magazine, June 1986.*

US Army Corps of Engineers. The Permafrost Tunnel in Fox, Alaska [brochure]. 2012.

THE EARTH RUMBLES AND BLOWS SMOKE

Hubbard, Bernard R. *Mush, You Malemutes!* New York: The America Press, 1938.

Judson, Katharine Berry. *Myths and Legends of Alaska.* Chicago: A. C. McClurg & Co., 1911.

Ringsmuth, Katherine Johnson. *Beyond the Moon Crater Myth.* Washington DC: United States Department of the Interior Government Printing Office, December 2007.

Schaaf, Jeanne M. *Witness: Firsthand Accounts of the Largest Volcanic Eruption in the Twentieth Century.* Anchorage: National Park Service Katmai National Park and Preserve/ Aniachak National Monument and Preserve, 2004.

Smelcer, John. *The Raven & the Totem.* Anchorage: Salmon Run, 1992.

Willoughby, Barrett. *Alaskans All.* Boston and New York: Houghton Mifflin, 1933.

DENALI: WHO CLIMBED IT? WHO DIDN'T?

Bright, Norman. "Billy Taylor: The Youngest Sourdough." In Cole, *The Sourdough Expedition.* Anchorage: Alaska Northwest Publishing Company, 1985.

Cook, Frederick A. "From the Top of the Continent" (abridged). In Sherwonit, *Denali, a Literary Anthology.* Seattle: The Mountaineers Books, 2000.

Farquhar, Francis. "The Verdict of History." In Cole, *The Sourdough Expedition.* Anchorage: Alaska Northwest Publishing Company, 1985.

Haigh, Jane. *Denali: Early Photographs of Our National Parks.* Whitehorse: Wolf Creek Books, 2000.

Sherwonit, Bill. "The Sourdough Expedition 1910." In Mergler, *The Last New Land.* Anchorage: Alaska Northwest Books, 1996.

Stuck, Hudson. "I Saw the Flagpole." In Cole, *The Sourdough Expedition.* Anchorage: Alaska Northwest Publishing Company, 1985.

Thompson, W. F. "The First Account of the Conquering of Mount McKinley; The Story Behind the Story." In Cole, *The Sourdough Expedition.* Anchorage: Alaska Northwest Publishing Company, 1985.

———. "Tom Lloyd's Story of the Pioneer Climb." In Cole, *The Sourdough Expedition.* Anchorage: Alaska Northwest Publishing Company, 1985.

Washburn, Bradford, and Cherici, Peter. *The Dishonorable Dr. Cook.* Seattle: The Mountaineers Books, 2001.

Wickersham, James. "The Sage of Kantishnam—Legends of Denali." In Sherwonit, *Denali, A Literary Anthology.* Seattle: The Mountaineers Books, 2000.

THE CACHE CREEK MURDERS: WHO DID IT? WHERE'S THE GOLD?

Belli, Anthony M. "Dark Deed—The Cache Creek Murders." *Lost Treasure,* January 2010: 52.

Sheldon, Roberta. *The Mystery of the Cache Creek Murders: A True Story.* Anchorage: Talkeetna Editions, 2001.

Wendt, Ron. *Haunted Alaska: Ghost Stories from the far North.* Kenmore: Epicenter Press, 2002.

THE MYSTERIOUS FLIGHT OF JAL 1628

Duke, Randy R. *U.F.O. Case Studies.* Wylie: M.C. Publishing, 2011.

Kean, Leslie. *UFOs.* New York: Three Rivers Press, 2010.

Maccabee, Bruce. *The Fantastic Flight of JAL 1628.* www .ufoevidence.org/documents/doc1316.htm.#FairUse.

INDEX

INDEX

Gavitt, Captain, 53–54
Gerken, Ted, 42–43
ghosts
  Bart Jacobsen and John, 31–33
  guiding fisherman, 31–33
  guiding lost ship. *See Eliza Anderson*
  guiding miner at sea, 29–30
  H. O./G. W. Blankenship and, 29–30
  Tom Wright and, 22, 23, 28
Gold Rush
  Eliza Anderson and, 23–24
  ghost-guided boat and, 29–30
  Kah Lituya and, 4–5
Guthrie, Dale, 81

hadrosaur fossils, 83–84
Hairy Man, 34–45
  ape-like sounds, 38, 44
  Brad Josephs and, 37–39
  demeanor, 44–45
  description, 34
  Dogfish Bay encounter, 39–40
  Ed Schlief and, 39–40
  footprints/tracks, 42–43, 44
  Greg Christian and, 40–42
  illustrated, 35
  J. Robert Alley and, 44–45
  Kayak Beach sightings, 41–42
  Lake Iliamna encounters, 42–43
  lake/river episodes, 37–38
  lore, 34–36
  Malania Kehl and, 36–37
  Port Chatham encounters, 36–37, 40–41
  Portlock encounter, 38–39
  Southeast stories and sightings, 44–45
  unanswered questions, 45
  various names of, 34, 44
  villages abandoned due to, 37
Hammersly, Bill, 47, 48, 54
Hansen, Christ, 115–16
Harper, Walter, 111
Hillstrand, Jonathon and Andy, 54
Holyoke. See Richard Holyoke
Hubbard, Father Bernard, 91–94
Huscroft, James, 5–6
Hutchison, Isobel Wylie, 11, 12, 18–19, 21

ice worms, 66–75
  characteristics, 71–74
  definition, 69–70
  dependence on ice, 74

documentation and displays, 71
entertainment based on, 74–75
fictional, genesis of, 68–69
gag story becomes mythical Ice Worms,
  68–70
government interest, 69–70
photograph, 72
real, discovery, 70–71
reducing numbers, 73–74
scientific name, 71
Stroller White and, 66–70
top authority on, 73–74
Iliamna, Lake, 46–55
  big fish/fishlike creatures. *See* "Illies"
  Hairy Man encounters, 42–43
  name origin, meaning, 46
  size, location, and access, 46–47
Iliamna volcano, 95, 97, 99
"Illies," 47–55
  cryptids and, 52, 54
  cryptozoology of, 48–49, 52
  dinosaur-age creature and, 55
  Nushagak Bay creature and, 54
  other gigantic sea creatures and, 53–54
  possible explanations, 50–53, 55
  seals and, 49–50
  sharks and, 50, 55
  sightings, searches, and descriptions,
    47–50, 54
  sturgeons and, 50–52
  Tizheruks and, 52–53
  whales and, 55
ircenrraats, 56–57, 59–62

Jacobsen, Bart, 31–33
JAL 1628 flight mystery, 128–39
  cargo and origin/destination, 128–29
  crew interviews and follow-up
    investigations, 134–39
  deviating from object, 132–33
  diagrams, 134–35
  flying conditions, 130
  initial UFOs sighted, 129
  later UFO sightings, 139
  "primary returns" and, 131–32, 133–34
  publicity about, 137–38
  radar readings, 129, 130–32, 133–34,
    138, 139
  silhouetted spaceship sighting, 132
  tracking UFO's lights, 129–32
  unanswered questions, 139

ABOUT THE AUTHOR

Cherry Lyon Jones, a Colorado College alumna, has been a preschool/parent education teacher, has owned and operated a children's bookstore, has done portrayals of historical women, and is a storyteller. A native Texan, she has spent her adult life in California and Nevada, and now, Ocala, Florida, in the winters, and Homer, Alaska, in the summers. History has always been her avocation and reading, her great pleasure. She belongs to the Society of Children's Book Writers and Illustrators and the Nevada Women's History Project.